THE ENGLISH REVOLUTION

1688–1689

THE ENGLISH REVOLUTION

1688–1689

G. M. TREVELYAN

OXFORD UNIVERSITY PRESS
LONDON   OXFORD   NEW YORK

OXFORD UNIVERSITY PRESS

London   Oxford   New York
Glasgow   Toronto   Melbourne   Wellington
Cape Town   Ibadan   Nairobi   Dar es Salaam   Lusaka   Addis Ababa
Delhi   Bombay   Calcutta   Madras   Karachi   Lahore   Dacca
Kuala Lumpur   Singapore   Hong Kong   Tokyo

First published by Oxford University Press, London, 1938
First issued as an Oxford University Press paperback, 1965
This reprint, 1972
Printed in the United States of America

CONTENTS

THE ENGLISH REVOLUTION

1688–1689

I   INTRODUCTORY

Why do historians regard the Revolution of 1688 as important? And did it deserve the title of "glorious" which was long its distinctive epithet? "The Sensible Revolution" would perhaps have been a more appropriate title and certainly would have distinguished it more clearly as among other revolutions.

But in so far as it was indeed "glorious," in what does its "glory" consist? It is not the Napoleonic brand of glory. It is not to be sought in the glamour of its events, the drama of its scenes, and the heroism of its actors, though these also rouse the imagination and stir the blood. The Seven Bishops passing to the Tower through the kneeling throngs; William's fleet floating into Torbay before the Protestant wind; the flight of James II, following his wife and infant son to France, none of them ever to return—doubtless these are romantic scenes, that live in memory. Such also are the events that followed more bloodily in Scotland and in Ireland—the roaring pass of Killie-crankie, the haggard watch on Londonderry walls, and Boyne water bristling with musket and pike. Yet all these are not, like the fall of the Bastille or Napoleon's Empire, a new birth of time, a new shape of terror. They are spirited variations on themes invented forty years before by a more heroic, creative and imprudent generation.

The Seven Bishops whom James II prosecuted were milder and more conservative men than the Five Members whom Charles I attempted to arrest, yet the second story reads much like a repetition of the first: in both cases the King rashly attacks popular leaders who are protected by the law, and by the mass opinion of the capital. In both cases the King's downfall shortly follows. Much else indeed is

3

very different: there is no English civil war on the second occasion, for in 1688 even the Cavaliers (renamed Tories) were against the King. But the men of the Revolution, James and William, Danby, Halifax, Sancroft, Dundee, are manipulating forces, parties and ideas which had first been evoked in the days of Laud, Strafford, Pym, Hampden, Hyde, Cromwell, Rupert, Milton and Montrose. In the later Revolution there are no new ideas, for even Toleration had been eagerly discussed round Cromwell's camp-fires. But in 1688 there is a very different grouping of the old parties, and a new and happier turn is given to the old issues, in England though not in Ireland, by compromise, agreement and toleration. An heroic age raises questions, but it takes a sensible age to solve them. Roundheads and Cavaliers, high in hope, had broken up the soil, but the Whigs and Tories soberly garnered the harvest.

A certain amount of disillusionment helps to make men wise, and by 1688 men had been doubly disillusioned, first by the rule of the Saints under Cromwell, and then by the rule of the Lord's Anointed under James. Above all, taught by experience, men shrank from another civil war. The burnt child fears the fire. The merit of this Revolution lay not in the shouting and the tumult, but in the still, small voice of prudence and wisdom that prevailed through all the din.

The true "glory" of the Revolution lies not in the minimum of violence which was necessary for its success, but in the way of escape from violence which the Revolution Settlement found for future generations of Englishmen. There is nothing specially glorious in the victory which our ancestors managed to win, with the aid of foreign arms, over an ill-advised King who forced an issue with nine-tenths of his English subjects on the fundamentals of law, politics and religion. To have been beaten at such odds would have been national ignominy indeed. The "glory" of that brief and bloodless campaign lies with William, who laid deep and complicated plans and took great risks in coming over at all, rather than with the English who had only to throw up their caps for him with sufficient unanimity when once he and his troops had landed. But it is England's true glory that the cataclysm of James's overthrow was not accompanied by the shedding of English blood either on the field or on the scaffold. The political instincts of our people appeared in the avoidance of a second civil war, for which all the elements were present. Our enemy Louis XIV of France had confidently expected that another long period of confusion and strife would ensue in our factious island if William should land there; if he had thought otherwise, he could have threatened the frontiers of Holland, and so prevented his rival from setting sail at all.

But the Convention Parliament of February 1689, by uniting England, baffled the policy of France. By wise compromise it stanched for ever the blood feud of Roundhead and Cavalier, of Anglican and Puritan, which had broken out first at Edgehill and Naseby, and bled afresh only four years back at Sedgemoor. Whig and Tory, having risen together in rebellion against James, seized the fleeting moment of their union to fix a new-old form of Government, known in history as the Revolution Settlement. Under it, England has lived at peace within herself ever since. The Revolution Settlement in Church and State proved to have the quality of permanence. It stood almost unaltered until the era of the Reform Bill of 1832. And throughout the successive stages of rapid change that have followed, its fundamentals have remained to bear the weight of the vast democratic superstructure which the nineteenth and twentieth centuries have raised upon its sure foundation. Here, seen at long range, is "glory," burning steadily for 250 years: it is not the fierce, short, destructive blaze of *la gloire*.

The expulsion of James was a revolutionary act, but otherwise the spirit of this strange Revolution was the opposite of revolutionary. It came not to overthrow the law but to confirm it against a law-breaking King. It came not to coerce people into one pattern of opinion in politics or religion, but to give them freedom under and by the law. It was at once liberal and conservative; most revolutions are neither one nor the other, but overthrow the laws, and then tolerate no way of thinking save one. But in our Revolution the two great parties in Church and State united to save the laws of the land from destruction by James; having done so, and having thereby become jointly and severally masters of the situation in February 1689, neither the Whig nor the Tory party would suffer its clients to be any longer subject to persecution, either by the Royal power or by the opposite party in the State. Under these circumstances the keynote of the Revolution Settlement was personal freedom under the law, both in religion and in politics. The most conservative of all revolutions in history was also the most liberal. If James had been over-

thrown either by the Whigs alone or by the Tories alone, the settlement that followed his downfall would not have been so liberal, or
so permanent.[1]

In the realm of thought and religion, individual liberty was secured by the abandonment of the cherished idea that all subjects of
the State must also be members of the State Church. The Toleration
Act of 1689 granted the right of religious worship, though not complete political equality, to Protestant Dissenters; and so strong was
the latitudinarian and tolerant spirit of the age ushered in by the
Revolution, that these privileges were soon extended in practice
though not in law to the Roman Catholics, against whom the Revolution had in one aspect been specially directed.

The political freedom of the individual was secured in a like spirit,
by the abolition of the Censorship (1695), by the milder and less
partial administration of political justice, and by the balance of
power between the Whig and Tory parties, under whose rival ban-
ners almost everyone in some sort found shelter. In these ways the
distinctively English idea of the freedom of opinion and the rights
of the individual were immensely enhanced by the peculiar character
of this Revolution.

James had tried to put the King above Parliament and above the
Law. The Revolution, while leaving the King the source of executive
authority, subjected him to the Law, which was henceforth to be interpreted by independent and irremovable Judges, and could only be
altered by Act of Parliament. At the same time, by the annual Mutiny
Act that made the army dependent of Parliament, and by the refusal
to grant to William for life the supplies that had been granted for
the lives of Charles and James II, the House of Commons obtained
a power of bargaining with Government that rendered it even more
important than the House of Lords; indeed, from the Revolution on-
wards the Commons gradually gained a control even over the executive power of the King, through the Cabinet system which grew up
step by step under William, Anne and the first two Georges. All this
was not foreseen by the men of 1689, whose intention was only to

---

[1] The remarks in this introduction refer to England alone. In Scotland, where
the Revolution in the winter of 1688 was made by the Presbyterian or Whig
party with little aid from the Episcopalians, the settlement of 1689 was one-
sidedly Presbyterian. And the result was that civil war remained endemic in
Scotland until 1746. In Ireland, the Revolution Settlement was a racial and
religious re-conquest of the most brutal kind.

subject the kingly power to the bounds of law as defined by the parliamentary lawyers. But the Hanoverian Constitution of Walpole and the Pitts grew straight out of the Revolution Settlement by the logic of experience.

The Revolution has been branded as aristocratic. It was effected by the whole nation, by a union of all classes; but in a society still mainly agricultural, where the economic and social structure rendered the landlords the natural and accepted leaders of the countryside, noblemen and squires like the Tories Danby and Seymour, the Whigs Devonshire and Shrewsbury took the lead when resistance to government had to be improvised. The nation indeed recognized no other chiefs through whom it could act in such an emergency. A similar aristocratic and squirearchical leadership of the country had organized both the Roundhead and Cavalier armies at the beginning of the Civil War; it had, indeed, been partially eclipsed during the rule of Cromwell's military saints, but had been fully re-established at the Restoration of 1660. It continued after 1689 as before, and would in any case have continued until the Industrial Revolution gradually raised up a new social order. Even Despotism, if James had succeeded in setting it up, must in that age have governed through nobles and squires. James attempted to use the lords and country gentlemen who were the Lieutenants and J.P.'s of their counties as the instruments of his Catholicizing policy, but they, like everyone else, turned against him. Having no other bureaucracy through which to work, he fell.

So far, the Revolution was indeed a demonstration of the power of the landlord classes, Whig and Tory alike. They were politically powerful because in the then formation of English Society they were indispensable. Any form of English government must in those days have worked through them.

The Revolution did quite as much for the legal, mercantile and popular elements in our national life as for the aristocratic or squirearchical. The worst permanent result of the Revolution was not the alleged increase in the power of the aristocracy but the undue conservatism that continued throughout the whole eighteenth century. The result of the reaction against James II's innovations was to put too great a stress, for many years to come, on the perpetuation of institutions in their existing form. James, in the interest of Roman Catholicism and Despotism, had remodelled the Town Corporations, invaded the liberties of the Universities and of the Church, and attempted to pack the House of Commons. In the rebound, the Ministries and Parliaments of the eighteenth century feared to reform the Corporations, Universities, Church benefices and Parliamentary Constituencies, even in the interest of purer and more efficient government. James had treated charters as waste paper, so the men of the eighteenth century regarded sheepskin with superstitious reverence. They held that whatever is is right—if it can show a charter. The hundred and fifty years that followed the Revolution are the most conservative in our annals though by no means the least free, happy or prosperous.

The Whig Governments before Burke, and the Tory Governments after him, all had too much reverence for the letter of the Revolution Settlement. It became a flag of ultra conservatism, first Whig then Tory. To Walpole, Blackstone, Burke, Eldon and the anti-Jacobin Tories of the early nineteenth century, the year 1689 seemed the last year of creation, when God looked upon England and saw that it was good.

But when this ultra-conservative mood at length passed away, the bases of the Revolution Settlement still remained as the foundations of the new era of rapid Reform, in which we are still living after more than a hundred years. The relation of the Crown to Parliament and to the Law; the independence of Judges; the annual meeting of Parliament; the financial supremacy of the Commons; the position of the Church of England; the Toleration of religious Dissent; freedom of political speech and writing subject to no control but the opinion of a jury; in short, a Constitutional Monarchy for a free people, these are the bases of our polity and they were well and truly laid by the Whigs and Tories, the nobles, squires, lawyers, merchants and populace who rose up against James II.

But unless strength upholds the free, freedom cannot live. And the Revolution Settlement gave us strength as well as freedom. The Marlborough wars soon demonstrated that; and England was never so safe and so powerful as in the eighteenth century, especially after the Parliamentary Union with Scotland, made in 1707, had united the whole island of Britain "on a Revolution basis."

Between the death of Elizabeth and the Revolution of 1688, the constant struggle between Parliament and King had rendered England weak in the face of the world, except during the few years when Cromwell had given her strength at a heavy price. Our civil broils had occupied our energies and attention; sometimes both the King and the statesmen of the Opposition were pensioners of France; always Parliament had been chary of supply to governments whose policy they could not continuously control. In the reigns of the Jameses and Charleses, foreign countries had regarded our Parliament as a source of weakness, hampering the executive power: the Constitution of England was contemptuously compared to that of Poland.

But after the Revolution the world began to see that our parliamentary government, when fully established, was capable of becoming a source of national strength. Supplies that had been refused to Kings whom the Commons could not trust, were lavished on Ministries that had the confidence of the House. The money must be voted afresh annually, not granted for the King's life; and the Commons must see to its appropriation. On these strict conditions, the governments of William, Anne and the Georges had the run of the national purse such as their predecessors had not enjoyed. Moreover, the "Revolution Governments" had the confidence of the City as well as of Parliament. The system of loans based on taxes gave England the key to power. It was "Revolution finance" and Revolution policy that enabled Marlborough to defeat the Grand Monarch, when free government and religious toleration triumphed over the revoker of the Edict of Nantes. As a result of that victory, the European philosophers of the eighteenth century turned against political despotism and religious intolerance as causes of national weakness, and proclaimed to the world the peculiar merits of England's "happy constitution in Church and State."

Speaking of the wars of William and Anne, and more generally of the eighteenth century, Professor G. N. Clark writes:

In France and Prussia and almost everywhere militarism and autocracy went hand in hand, but what enabled Britain to deploy its strength was the Revolution Settlement. The main lines of policy were laid down by a small gathering of Ministers who had at their disposal full departmental information about foreign affairs, finance, military and naval preparations and trade. By means of parliament the Ministers brought into the service of that policy the wealth and manpower of the nation. . . . Parliament was a meeting-place where divergent economic interests were reconciled and combined so as to provide an adequate body of support for the government of the day.[1]

[1] "The Later Stuarts," by Professor G. N. Clark, in the *Oxford History of England*, 1934.

In this way Britain obtained, not only political and religious liberty, but national power, greater than that of the unlimited monarchy of France. Such are the reasons why modern historians regard the Revolution a turning-point in the history of our country and of the world.

Before anyone can profitably study the events of James II's reign and the Revolution Settlement which they produced, he must ask some first questions. What had been happening in Church and State in the previous quarter of a century? And what was the condition of parties and opinion when James came to the throne?

The reign of Charles II from 1660 to 1685 may be viewed, in one of its many aspects, as the failure of the Restoration Settlement permanently to settle the English Constitution. Not that the Restoration Settlement was in the main a failure: its supreme merit was that it liquidated the Cromwellian revolutionary period with a minimum of bloodshed and reprisals, and restored King, Parliament and the rule of Law in place of armed force. But the temporary appeasement of parties and the restoration of the rule of Law were attained by the only means possible in 1660, namely, by establishing an equilibrium between Crown and Parliament, which postponed the ultimate trial of strength between the monarchical and the representative principle. That equilibrium was believed by Clarendon to be the summit of political wisdom, the true and final balance of our Constitution. No more Strafford and no more Pym! It was a lawyer's idea of politics, with all the merits and defects of a lawyer's idea. Crown and Parliament are neither to be trusted far. Law and custom are to prescribe the limits of the power of each, which neither is to outstep. Excellent! But what if Crown and Parliament were to quarrel? Who then should decide, and how should a growing country and a growing Empire be guided and governed by two semi-sovereign powers perpetually at variance? The equilibrium between Crown and Parliament, invaluable for a few years of restoration work, could not be a permanent settlement. It soon led to quarrels between the two co-ordinate powers, in the first instance between Charles II and his own Cavalier Parliament, elected in the fever of royalist enthusiasm that followed his return from exile. That quarrel sealed the doom of Clarendon and of his system of politics (1667).

Mr. Arthur Bryant has recently written a brilliant and attractive book on Charles II. It puts the case for him admirably and corrects previous unfair estimates. Mr. Bryant is a fine biographer, but I think he hardly realizes the seriousness of the French danger in Europe at that time, which Charles II's Treaty of Dover policy (1670) greatly increased. Moreover, Mr. Bryant is not interested in Constitutional history, and does not see the point of view necessarily taken by any House of Commons in face of Royal power. The Cavalier Parliament kept Charles short of money, not from mere wantonness, but because it could not control his expenditure and did not trust his policy; the secret Treaty of Dover has shown to posterity that this want of confidence was amply justified. Till the House of Commons could supervise the use of the money it voted—as it did after the Revolution—it was hopeless to expect even a Cavalier Parliament to vote enough for the real needs of the nation. For if Parliament had voted money freely before it had control of expenditure, it would never have become the supreme power in the State and must have sunk back into its old position under the Tudors. No Parliament, however Cavalier or Tory, would vote to Charles or James II enough money to conduct a vigorous policy at home and abroad, because no Parliament could exert continuous control over the decision what that policy was to be.

The Restoration Settlement was a provisional compromise between kingly and parliamentary power, and had the disadvantages as well as the advantages of compromise. Under such a system of divided authority, England could neither have been strongly governed at home, nor have maintained her sea power, world-wide trade and Empire in the face of the growing power of France. Before she could move forward to her destiny, she had first either to become a despotism with royal control of taxation like her rivals oversea, or else to develop into a new form of polity, such as the world had never yet seen, a State in which the House of Commons would dictate the policy of the King and his Ministers. After the Revolution of 1688 had decided that the latter of these two paths was to be taken, the national purse strings were liberally opened year after year by the Commons to governments whom they could trust and control.

It is significant that this issue had emerged in the time of the Cavalier Parliament (1660-78). During those years the Cavalier or Tory party,[1] having the House of Commons as its instrument, stood up for parliamentary rights and powers against the King hardly less effectually than Pym, Hampden and the Roundhead leaders of old. Though bitterly hostile to Puritanism and the religious policy of the Long Parliament, the Cavalier-Tory squires took up the political testament of that famous Assembly, and constituted themselves the Parliamentary Party in opposition to the Court.

In domestic affairs, the chief quarrel between the Cavalier Parliament and Charles II arose on the matter of Religious Toleration. In order to understand the reigns of Charles and of his brother after him, it is necessary to keep in view the nature of the religious settlement of the Restoration, which was modified but not overthrown at the Revolution.

Indeed, for the next 200 years English politics turned largely on successive struggles for the repeal, maintenance and modification of the ecclesiastical settlement of 1660. Until the later years of Queen Victoria, Tory and Whig meant, more than anything else, the rival interest of Church and Dissent.

The Restoration Settlement caused the Established Church to be Anglican once more instead of Puritan, restored its endowments and privileges, and secured to its members the monopoly of State and Municipal office, of the two Universities and of the right to teach in schools. Moreover, religious services other than those of the Anglican Church were punished as criminal. The prison doors closed on Dissenting Ministers like Baxter and John Bunyan, the author of *Pilgrim's Progress*. Congregations could only meet in peril and by stealth. These harsh laws, passed between 1662 and 1665, are commonly known as the Clarendon Code: but, in fact, the Cavalier Parliament of Anglican squires were more responsible for its provisions than Clarendon, and were very much more responsible than Clarendon's easygoing master.

[1] It is impossible to state a difference, except of date, between Cavalier and Tory. It was during the Exclusion Bill struggle of 1679–81 that the name Tory took the place of Cavalier, and name Whig displaced that of Roundhead.

Charles II had none of that heat of religious zeal which led so many of his contemporaries to commit cruelty for Christ's sake. His Catholicism, like the Protestantism of Queen Elizabeth and Henry of Navarre, was the result of circumstance and experience, not a passion of the soul, and was tempered by scepticism bordering on infidelity. It was his policy to strengthen the power of the Crown against the overwhelming power of the Church party in the Cavalier Parliament, by giving relief to Dissenters, Catholic and Protestant alike, through the Royal Prerogative of dispensing with the laws, to which he laid claim. He thus hoped to preserve the Dissenters as his humble clients and vassals, very much as the mediæval kings used for their own ends to preserve the Jews from popular malice. Moreover, Charles wished to protect the Roman Catholics, as he owed his life to Catholic loyalty after Worcester, and, so far as he had any religion, was himself a crypto-Catholic. But he knew that he would not be permitted to protect the Catholics unless he also protected the Protestant Dissenters. So he issued Declarations of Indulgence, partially suspending the operation of the persecuting laws by right of his royal prerogative. The Cavalier Parliament challenged these Declarations as unconstitutional: it was, they declared, beyond the King's power to interfere with the operation of Acts of Parliament. Charles, in need of money and of quiet, gave way to the Commons and withdrew the Declaration of Indulgence as having been unlawful (1672-3). Constitutional Liberty had won a great battle at the expense of Religious Toleration. This claim to suspend the laws, which Charles had been forced to abandon, was, as we shall see, afterwards revived by James II in a more wholesale fashion, and with more memorable results.

The Clarendon Code and its enforcement must therefore be ascribed not to the House of Stuart, but to the House of Commons. The motive was not primarily religious persecution. The squires of England at the Restoration were eager for political vengeance, not for religious propaganda. They persecuted heresy indeed, but not in order to save the Puritans' souls—they would not have crossed the street to do that—but to prevent them from rising again to overthrow the Church, behead the King and confiscate the property of the squires. "Never again" was the attitude of the Cavalier Parliament to the Puritans. It was for this reason that they passed a long series of measures against religious nonconformity; it seemed to them the only available means of permanently depressing the Roundhead party and preventing another swing of the pendulum which might again overturn throne and altar. From an Anglican point of view, parts of this legislation can be defended in the circumstances of the time; other parts must be condemned by any reasonable man; but all of it was very natural. It was not an unprovoked piece of cruelty like Louis XIV's Revocation of the Edict of Nantes. It was dictated, not by religious fanaticism, but by fear based on recent and cruel experience.

After the Puritan peril came the Roman Catholic peril. Towards the end of the Cavalier Parliament, at the time of the Treaty of Dover and the last Dutch War, the danger of Roman Catholicism in high places again became apparent. The chief influences at Court, the King's most trusted Ministers, his brother and heir, his Queen and the majority of his mistresses were all Catholic, and his foreign policy was dictated by Catholic sympathies. The Test Act was therefore passed in 1673 to defend the Church of England on that side also. It was not repealed till 1828-9. The Test Act made it illegal for anyone to hold civil or military office unless he had first taken the sacrament according to the rites of the Church of England. This method of employing a religious rite as a political test, highly and properly distasteful to modern notions, was adopted because it was regarded as the only perfectly effective means of keeping Roman Catholics out of office. Oaths and declarations were not enough; in that age they were always being imposed, and were lightly taken and lightly broken by men of all parties and all faiths. But no Roman Catholic would take part in an heretical sacrament. And so the Sacramental Test for 150 years served its purpose by keeping out of office all Roman Catholics; and incidentally it kept out many Protestant Nonconformists as well, though some of these latter had no objection to taking the Anglican sacrament, and were called "occasional conformists."

One of the first results of the Test Act of 1673 was to drive from office James, Duke of York, the heir to the throne. But, though no post under the Crown might any longer be held by a Romanist, the accession to the Crown itself was not yet subjected to a similar limitation. James, though he could no longer preside over the Admiralty, would some day ascend the throne; and when that day came the observance or breach of the Test Act was certain to become the chief issue between him and his Protestant subjects.

But though the Cavalier-Tory Parliament had opposed Charles II in his policy of Toleration for Protestant and Catholic Dissenters at

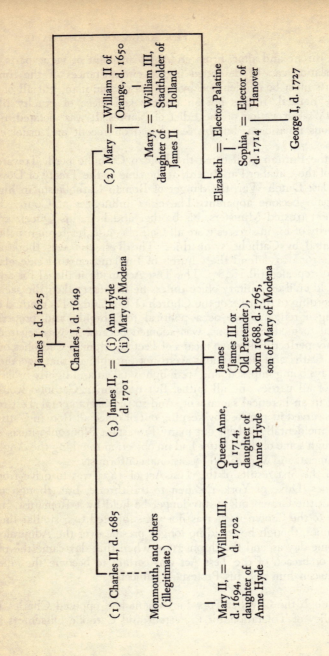

home, and in his pro-French policy abroad, his quarrel with that party never became as bitter as his quarrel with the three Whig Parliaments that followed (1679-81). For the Tories were after all the sons of the Cavaliers who had fought for the Crown, and the Whigs were the sons of the Roundheads. When therefore the violent conduct of the Whig Parliaments under Shaftesbury in the second half of Charles II's reign seemed to revive the old issues and passions of the Civil War, all the instincts of the Tory squires and clergy bade them rally round the throne with heart and soul.

The two parties were indeed divided not merely by the degree of their opposition to the Royal power, but yet more fundamentally on religion. The Tories were Anglican "High Churchmen," who sought to depress Protestant Dissenters by enforcing the Clarendon Code, and so extirpate Puritanism as well as Catholicism from an island that should be wholly Anglican. The Whigs were a combination of latitudinarian "Low Churchmen" with Puritan Dissenters to defend the Nonconformist Sects against persecution, and possibly some day to turn the tables once more against the Anglican Church. Both Whig and Tory were against the Roman Catholics, but whenever the No Popery cry was loudest, the Whigs benefited most, because ordinary Churchmen then forgot their fear of the Puritan Dissenters.

The quarrel between Whigs and Tories in the last years of Charles II's reign had therefore many deep-seated causes, but it came to a head on the Exclusion Bill, by which the Whigs proposed to exclude from the succession to the throne the King's brother James, then Duke of York. The half-revealed Treaties of Dover and the Dutch War of 1672 in alliance with Louis XIV, had alarmed Protestants of all parties as to the growth of Roman Catholic and French influences at Court. In 1678 James's secretary, Coleman, was caught corresponding with the confessor of Louis XIV on a plan for the extirpation of Protestantism in England by the help of France. These "Coleman letters," the genuine appendage of the sham Popish Plot of Titus Oates, had been published with terrible effect and partly accounted for public credulity in Oates' infamous inventions. There was a real Popish Plot; it was latent in the bosom of the heir to the throne, and it emerged six years later when James was King.

He would never have become King had not the Tory or Anglican party rallied to the side of strict hereditary succession. In the struggle over the Exclusion Bill in three successive Parliaments (1679-81) the Whig and Tory parties took their permanent form and found their famous names. In pressing for the exclusion of James, the Whigs showed themselves more in the right than their opponents as to his suitability to fill the throne, and more far-seeing as to the impossibility of a zealous Roman Catholic exercising, as King, the duties and prerogatives of head of the English State and principal patron and governor of the English Church. Ten years later, the Tories were fain to join in turning off the throne the very man whom they had placed there, and in passing a law that no Roman Catholic should ever again be King of England. But in other respects the Whigs went far astray. Under Lord Shaftesbury's leadership, the cynical levity of Restoration statesmen seemed added to the forceful fanaticism of the old Roundheads. The party was as far as possible from the moderation afterwards associated with the Whig name by Somers and Walpole.

Not content with excluding James, the Whig chiefs flirted with the idea of causing Charles's bastard, Monmouth, to be made heir to the throne. It would be fine to have a Whig party leader as King. To accomplish this, some of the Whigs were ready to pass over the legitimate claims of James's Protestant daughters Mary and Anne, and of Mary's husband, William of Orange, who had a somewhat more distant claim to the throne in his own right also.

The interest of William and Mary was, in those days, left to the championship of the Tory, Danby. The Whigs had not yet realized, except occasionally for purposes of party propaganda, the danger from the overgrown power of France, and the consequent necessity for England to be friends with William and with Holland. Some of the Whig chiefs were in the pay of France, no less than the King whom they opposed. At the time of the Popish Plot and Exclusion Bill, the two English statesmen who fully grasped the true relation of our domestic policy to affairs abroad, were Sir William Temple, the diplomatist, and Lord Danby, the Tory leader. They both saw that England and Holland must stand together against France, or both would be subjected to her hegemony. It was for that reason that Danby had, in a fortunate hour, arranged the marriage between William of Orange, the Dutch Stadtholder, and James's Protestant daughter Mary, her father's presumptive heir (1677). This marriage, a stroke of the truest statesmanship, proved in the end the undoing of Louis XIV's plans of world-conquest, for it served as the dynastic foundation of the Revolution Settlement.

But next year (1678), Danby fell under a cloud, and Temple had no political courage. For a while William's interest was neglected by all parties in England. The Whigs suspected the autocratic traditions of the Orange family which had always been opposed to the Republican party in Holland: many of them preferred the prospect of "King Monmouth's" accession. The Tories looked forward with equal delight to the prospect of the reign of James. Moderation and prudence were forgotten in the fierce party fight with which the reign of Charles II closed. Tories and Whigs proceeded to throw away England's best interests at home and abroad, in a rivalry of folly which boded ill for the future of the two-party system. Indeed, the prestige of parliamentary government as a possible form of polity was gravely lowered, in the eyes of Europe and of England, by the proceedings of Shaftesbury's three Whig Parliaments from 1679 to 1681. Their cruelties against Roman Catholics, at the time of the Popish Plot, helped to stimulate the more systematic and long-continued persecution of the Huguenots in France. The support many of them gave to the claims of the worthless bastard Monmouth to the English throne, and the reckless character of the inroads made by the House of Commons on the executive and judicial spheres, these proceedings of the Whigs alarmed moderate men. It seemed that "1641 was come again" and that another civil war was fast approaching. People were then as anxious to avoid another civil war as we to-day are anxious to avoid another foreign war. To avoid that pit of calamity, men rallied round the throne. In 1681 the Whig power was broken, and with it fell the power of Parliament, until seven years later the events of the Revolution revived it in a more stable and satisfactory form.

Charles, who in his cynical, good-natured fashion was a very able politician, though not a constructive statesman, gave the Whigs rope enough, and by 1681 they had fairly hanged themselves. Then the Tories took up the tale of wrongdoing. They prepared an evil day for the Church of their devotion, for they lavished on the Crown powers which were about to be inherited, as a result of their own action, by one of the most bigoted Roman Catholics in Europe. They helped the Crown to destroy the independent charters of the Municipal Corporations, which had many of them been Whig, on the assumption that in the hands of the Crown the Municipalities would henceforth always be Tory. They helped to establish a Royalist terror in the land. In the days of the Cavalier Parliament in the previous decade, the Tories, as we have seen, had been a parliamentary party, and they were soon to be so again. But for a few years, from 1680 to 1685, in their rage against Shaftesbury and his Whig Parliaments they became a party of Courtiers. The real tradition, genius and power of the Tory party lay in its action as a parliamentary party. At bottom they were not in favour of absolutism, yet they now behaved and talked as if they were. This was their great aberration, the ill consequences of which to themselves were not finally exhausted till after the middle of the eighteenth century.[1]

To their own eventual undoing, the Tories proclaimed, as an essential part of the Anglican Church teaching, the doctrine of the divine hereditary right of kings, coupled with the doctrine of non-resistance in its extreme form. Their divines declared and their politicians repeated that no tyranny, however illegal or cruel, could ever justify a subject in resisting the hereditary monarch in arms, because hereditary monarchy was of divine origin. Oxford University in 1683 issued a manifesto officially proclaiming the doctrine of unconditional non-resistance "as in a manner the badge or doctrine of the Church of England." The parish pulpits resounded with it. Events were soon to show whether the doctrine would be fatal to English liberty—or only to Tory logic.

The conduct of Whigs and Tories between 1678 and 1685 is so mad and bad that it is a psychological puzzle to recognize any of the better elements usually found in the English political character—humanity, decency or common sense. Whigs and Tories act like the nervous and hot-blooded factions of a South European race. They rant, scream, bully, assassinate men by forms of law, study no interest but their own, and betray even their own interest through sheer folly and passion. Yet, a few years later, these same men took part in making and observing the Revolution Settlement, the most English thing that ever was done—if, indeed, it is English to take stand on good sense, compromise and toleration. Part of the explanation lies in the exemplary punishment that in good time fell on both parties, as a direct and evident consequence of the faults that each had committed. The political leaders of that period were at least clever men, and they learnt in the school of adversity. The reforma-

[1] Such is the theme of the modern historiographer of the Tory party, Mr. Keith Feiling of Oxford, whose volume *The History of the Tory Party, 1640–1714*, speaks with more intimacy and authority than I can claim to do about Tory faith and fortunes, but I disagree with none of his main contentions.

tion of Whigs and Tories and their conversion to political sanity was the greatest of the unintentional achievements of James II.

But indeed the most violent and unscrupulous leaders on both sides, Shaftesbury, Sunderland and Jeffreys, disappeared from the scene either before or during the Revolution of 1688. The men who took the leading part in the making of the Revolution Settlement, Tories like Danby and Nottingham, Whigs like Shrewsbury and Devonshire, Trimmers like Halifax, had none of them been guilty of the worst excesses of party spirit in previous years. There had always been a residuum of political good sense to be found somewhere, even in the last years of Charles's reign, and it was found at its strongest in the wit and wisdom of George Savile, Marquis of Halifax, "the Trimmer," the Philosopher Statesman, whose dislike of extremes always caused him to "trim" away from whichever party was at the moment enjoying and abusing power.

The last four years of the reign of Charles were years of peace after the storms of the Popish Plot and Exclusion Bill. It was a peace not of agreement, but of conquest. The Whigs were crushed apparently beyond hope of revival. The insurrection plot of some of their chiefs and the Rye House Plot of some of their under-strappers to murder the royal brothers (1683), only served to complete the ruin of the party and to increase the popular execration of everything Puritan and of everything Whig. The press was muzzled by the Censorship, and words spoken or written against the existing order were cruelly punished by judges and juries as prejudiced against Whigs and Dissenters as they had been a few years back against Roman Catholics. The principal Whig chiefs paid the penalty of their violence and folly on the scaffold, like Russell and Sidney, or, like Shaftesbury, by death in exile. The remaining lords and gentlemen of the party were living retired, each in his own country seat, far from Court and City, glad to be spared at the price of complete retirement from public life. Their clients, the Protestant Dissenters, who formed the rank and file of the Whig party, were again persecuted with the utmost rigour of the Clarendon Code, while the persecuting laws against Roman Catholics again slept. By terrorism, collusion or by very doubtful processes of law, the Town Corporations were compelled or induced to surrender their independent charters, and to take instead new charters at the King's will. These remodelled Corporations were filled with Tories and Royalists. If Parliament were now to be summoned, the House of Commons would be Tory and Royalist by an overwhelming majority, for not only was public opinion against the Whigs, not only was the Whig organization dissolved, but the electoral bodies of many Parliamentary Boroughs had been packed by the same process as the Municipal Corporations.

Charles could have had a House of Commons after his own heart, but during the last four years of his reign he preferred not to meet the Houses at all. Since the Restoration there had been no such gap in the summons of Parliament, which was in fact illegal by the terms of the Triennial Act of 1664. It shows how far the balance of the Constitution had swayed back to the Monarchical side.

Since Charles let Parliament fall into abeyance, he could no longer obtain fresh annual supply. Yet it was not necessary for him to resort to illegal taxation; by strict economy he managed to live on the large grants which the Cavalier Parliament had made him for life at the beginning of his reign, supplemented by the gold of Louis XIV. So long as the King governed without Parliament, England could not, for financial reasons, take her place as head of the concert of smaller powers, Catholic and Protestant, who were endeavouring to restrain the advance of the French Monarch to hegemony over Europe. The question of our foreign policy was therefore closely allied to the question whether the King should govern with or without Parliament.

The party at Court, in these last years of Charles's reign, which desired to co-operate with a Parliament and oppose France was headed by Halifax the "Trimmer," who had earned the gratitude of the Tories and Royalists by leading the opposition to the Whig designs on the floor of the House of Lords in the late Parliaments. But Halifax had not succeeded in persuading Charles to summon Parliament and oppose France, when on February 6, 1685, the King's death changed the whole situation.

James II succeeded his brother, unchallenged and loudly acclaimed. For five years past he had been even more popular than Charles with the more violent Tories, whose custom it was to drink his health on their knees with the loud "Huzzah" which they had adopted as their party cry. The mere fact that the Whigs had tried to exclude James from the throne made him the idol of the more unthinking of the Tories. They felt sure that he would, even more

than his brother, serve their ends as a true Tory King. They opti-
mistically supposed that the powers they conferred on him would
still be used by the Crown, as in the last years of Charles II, to up-
hold the Church and the Tories and to crush the Dissenters and the
Whigs. That they themselves would ever feel any temptation to resist the Lord's Anointed never occurred to them, for they had reso-
lutely closed their eyes, for several years past, to two problems—the
position of the Roman Catholics in England, and the French hegemony in Europe. These two problems were bound to be brought to the
front together by King James, whose favourite advisers were Jesuits
of the French party and whose source of non-Parliamentary supply
was the gold of Louis XIV, the Revoker of the Edict of Nantes and
the would-be conqueror of Holland. The Roman Catholic and the
French question were one in Western Europe, and England could
not escape their repercussion now that James was on the throne. The
union of a Roman Catholic zealot, as King of England, with Louis
of France would, if long continued, have gravely endangered not
only the confessional independence of England, Holland the Protestant Churches of Europe, but also the political independence of all
European States. Therefore, Spain and the Roman Catholic Emperor,
and even the Pope as an Italian Prince, aligned themselves with the
Dutch and German Protestant States under William's banner, in
common cause against Louis and his vassal James. The decisive fac-
tor in the coming European crisis would be the action of the English
people, who understood little or nothing of the politics of Europe,
but were quick to take alarm whenever their own religion and liberties were attacked.

(The fullest modern history of the reign will be found in *England
in the Reign of Charles II*, by David Ogg, Fellow of New College,
Oxford Press, 1934, 2 vols.)

III   THE REIGN OF JAMES II

Such then was the state of parties and of opinion when James II succeeded to the throne in 1685. We now come to the strange events of his reign, which in three years fused the existing elements of politics into an entirely new combination, and kept them there at melting-point until the Revolution Settlement of 1689 emerged as the solid and permanent residuum of the crisis.

The four years of reaction, closing with the death of Charles II, had obscured the real crux of politics, that no logical process could reconcile the Tory political theory [of divine right of kings and non-resistance] with their constitutional sense and their religious convictions. The rule of Charles's successor was destined to strip off the intercepting veils of enthusiasm, and to leave this inconsistency naked, repulsive and challenging.

So writes the historian of the Tory Party.[1] But for the first few months of the reign the honeymoon was undisturbed. James, on the very day he became King, made a declaration in the Privy Council, which was printed and circulated to the joy of all true Tories and Englishmen: "I have been reported to be a man of arbitrary power, but that is not the only story that has been made of me; I shall make it my endeavour to preserve the government in Church and State as it is now by law established. I know the principles of the Church of England are for Monarchy. Therefore I shall always take care to defend and support it."

How could the happy and triumphant loyalists doubt that he

[1] Keith Feiling, *History of the Tory Party, 1640–1714*, p. 203.

would keep this solemn promise to observe the laws of the land and to support the Anglican Establishment? Strange as it may seem in the retrospect, James, at the time of his accession, was popularly reputed "a man of his word."

The new King's first step was to summon a Parliament. Until a House of Commons had voted him the revenues for life which his brother had enjoyed, he could not carry on the government even with help from the coffers of the King of France. Moreover, he had no desire to be the vassal of Louis, though he might wish to be his friend; and if he remained on good terms with Parliament he would be able to adopt an independent attitude in European affairs. That no doubt would please his subjects. He believed that he could be friends with a High Tory House of Commons. He thought that Tory principles would make them support him in everything, even in his schemes on behalf of the Roman Catholics. He desired that Parliament should repeal the Test Act and the Habeas Corpus Act and other laws that hampered his executive action. Then he could proceed, without any breach of the law, to fill up the Army, the Navy, the Cabinet and the Civil Service and the best places in the Church with his own co-religionists, side by side with High Anglicans. The Church pulpits would be tuned not to preach against "the King's religion"; and Puritanism would be extirpated by the continued application of the Clarendon Code against Protestant Dissenters. In that way the evolution of Church and State towards the Roman model could move peacefully forward.

Such was James II's first plan. The return to Rome was to be carried out with the half-conscious consent of the Church of England and with the active help of a Tory Parliament. It was only their refusal to oblige that led him to adopt another line to the same end, to break the laws, to attack the Church and the party that had placed him on the throne, and to court instead a chimerical alliance with the Puritan Dissenters, who bitterly hated both him and his religion.

In the last days of May 1685 James's Parliament met. Since the Town Corporations had been remodelled by arbitrary power at the end of the last reign, the new House of Commons was more carefully packed in the royal interest than any other with which any Stuart King had to deal. Sir Edward Seymour, the type and leader of the independent Tory country gentleman, complained of the way Government had interfered in the elections. At any rate there were only some forty members who were not either Tories or Courtiers.

The King repeated to Parliament the promises he had made to the Privy Council, to preserve the laws and to defend and support the Church of England. As yet he said nothing of the Repeal of the Test Act and Habeas Corpus Act, but demanded, in peremptory terms, the grant for his life of those revenues which had been voted for life to his brother. If any members thought of putting him on financial rations—"feeding me from time to time"—"I will answer once for all, that this would be a very improper way to take with me." He must have the revenues for life.

The High Tory House of Commons, deceived by his promises to support the Church of England, was loyalist enough to fall straight into the trap, and to vote him the Customs revenues for life. This enabled him, as soon as he had quarrelled with Parliament, to live without it for three fateful years. His financial independence proved, in fact, his political undoing, by tempting him along the road of tyranny. After the Revolution, this mistaken generosity on the part of the Commons was never repeated. No King or Queen has, since 1685, ever had a large revenue voted for life, and consequently no year since 1688 has passed without the meeting of Parliament.

At this stage, before King and Commons came to grips over the Test Act and the religious questions that were certain to divide them, the situation was profoundly altered by the Western Rebellion. The Duke of Monmouth was the foolish, handsome, bad young man, who had been put forward by the Shaftesbury Whigs in the days of their power as their candidate for the throne, on the strength of a lying tale that Charles II had been married to Monmouth's mother. Charles, though he loved the scamp better than any of his other natural children, did not recollect the ceremony, and declared he had rather see him dead than on the throne. If Monmouth had ever been made King by his partisans, his reign would have been as troubled and brief as that of James, and its catastrophe might well have had consequences fatal to the constitutional liberties of the land.

After the fall of his Whig patrons, Monmouth had retired to Holland. The Stadtholder, William of Orange, advised him to go off to the Danube and fight there for the Emperor against the Turk, turning his back on England. The ambitions of the two men were opposed; Monmouth's claim to the throne would bar the legitimate reversionary right of William's wife Mary to succeed her father James on the English throne. For that reason the Dutch Republican enemies of the Stadtholder took up his rival's cause. The magistrates of Amsterdam, to spite William and contrary to his orders, allowed the adventurer to charter a ship and load it with ammunition. With a few companions he landed at Lyme Regis (June 1685) in the South-West, where the Puritan peasantry and clothiers felt for their "King Monmouth" a romantic and fatal passion, akin to the feeling of Highland tribesmen in later years for "Bonnie Prince Charlie."

The Whig lords and gentlemen lay low in their country seats, but some 6,000 of the humbler classes in Somerset and Devon, especially in the Taunton clothing district, flocked to Monmouth's standard. The movement may be regarded as the last "peasants' rising" in England, though its motive was not social but religious. The sufferings of the Puritans under the Clarendon Code was a principal cause of the Rebellion. It was made in favour of the former Whig candidate for the throne, but its spirit was not so much Whig as a last flash of the old Roundhead fervour, *in extremis* and without the leadership and discipline that had made Cromwell's legions formidable. The object was to overthrow not only the Popish King but the Anglican Church. There was no smallest chance of success. Monmouth's brave followers were a mob, almost unofficered and imperfectly armed; they were not by nature and upbringing men of war like the Highlanders of 1745; many of them marched to their fate with no weapon but a scythe blade tied on a pole.

All the military elements were on the side of law and order. Even the militia of the two rebel counties stood by the King, as well as the more formidable regular troops. The parties and persons who united against James in 1688 were united against Monmouth in 1685. William of Orange lent his father-in-law three Scottish regiments in Dutch pay. The City of London and the two Houses of Parliament, the Universities, the Corporations, the rural magistrates and gentlemen, the opinion of the country were all for the King and the Law. The Tories were enthusiastic, the Whigs quiescent. Even a victory in the field would not have rallied any serious forces to Monmouth's side. If he had advanced out of the south-western area, he would have found the whole country against him. The romantic gallantry of the peasants and weavers against hopeless odds in the night battle on Sedgemoor, and the cruelties afterwards inflicted on them should not blind posterity to the utter wrongness as well as the folly of their rebellion.

The execution of Monmouth on Tower Hill was a punishment richly deserved. Of his followers, several hundreds were executed either by the soldiers after the battle or by the process of law at the "Bloody Assize," and about 800 more were sold as slaves to the Barbados. The grant of prisoners to individual favourites at Court to sell as slaves oversea was regarded by many Tory gentlemen as indecent. The atmosphere of the traffic at Court was already beginning to stink in their nostrils. Public opinion was shocked at the number of executions, and by the conduct of Judge Jeffreys on the Bench. The villages and towns of the South-West were made noisome by the gibbeted remains of the poor foolish lads. Most of all, men blamed the burning alive of Elizabeth Gaunt, and the beheading of Alice Lisle, both women of high character, guilty only of the sheltering of fugitives, an act of womanly mercy which was never punished with death by any other English Government in that or any subsequent century. The best elements in the Tory party and the Anglican Church disliked the Bloody Assize. Ken, the saintly Bishop of Bath and Wells, whose cathedral had been barbarously desecrated and injured by the Puritan rebels, exerted himself to save them from going in droves to the gallows. The distaste with which Jeffreys was now regarded by many Tories was doubled when he shortly afterwards betrayed the laws and the Church for royal favour.

Meanwhile, an even less successful attempt was made by the Earl of Argyle to evoke a rising in Scotland. His capture and execution relieved James of his most formidable enemy in the north of the island, for Argyle had combined the leadership of the Scottish Presbyterian party in the Lowlands with the chieftainship of the great Campbell Clan beyond the Highland line.

By the autumn of 1685 James had concentrated in his own hands all the elements of power in Great Britain. All his enemies were dead or at his feet. Yet in fact, the rebellions of Monmouth and Argyle, just because they added to his strength, lured him to his ruin. The ease with which the risings had been crushed, without receiving any support save from a few western fanatics, gave him an exaggerated idea of the loyalty of the land, which he considered absolute, whereas it was only contingent. Above all, the rebellion enabled him to raise and keep on foot a large regular army of some 30,000 men, on whom he imagined that he could depend to carry out the strange policies on which he presently embarked. And while these things encouraged him to defy the opinion of his subjects, the way to their ultimate union against him was cleared by the disappearance of Monmouth from the scene. Henceforth William of

Orange remained as the one possible champion of English religion and liberty, infinitely more formidable than Monmouth on account of his character and wisdom, his military and naval resources in Holland, his alliances in Europe, his wife's and his own legitimate nearness to the succession, and the fact that they were on terms at least as friendly with the Tories as with the Whigs.

November 1685 was the date of the second and last session of James's only Parliament. No more fateful session has ever been held at Westminster. Monmouth's rebellion had redoubled Tory zeal for James in the summer, but the autumn of the Bloody Assize had been full of sinister rumours that gravely disturbed Tory opinion. European Protestantism had its back to the wall; in October Louis XIV revoked the Edict of Nantes and waged an unprovoked and cruel war of extirpation against Protestantism among his French subjects, many of whom came flying to England, each with a tale of intolerable outrage. And in that same month, before the meeting of Parliament, there was an alarming increase of Roman Catholic influence in the counsels of the English King. The "Trimmer" Halifax was dismissed from office in October for his staunch adherence to the principle of the Test Act; and even more courtierlike High Churchmen such as Lords Rochester, Guildford and Clarendon were losing power. Their place in the innermost royal counsels was taken by Sunderland and Jeffreys, who would serve any purpose of the King in order to outbid their more scrupulous rivals. Sunderland had not yet apostatized, but he was already plotting against the Protestant interest with the Jesuit Father Petre and other Roman Catholics of the extreme party, who considered the moderating advice of the Pope as foolishness. Meanwhile, the great army raised to suppress Monmouth's rebellion was still on foot and the King avowed the intention of keeping it in permanence. Worst of all a large number of its officers were Roman Catholics, holding their commissions contrary to the law. Were dragonnades intended in England as well as in France?

Fear of a standing army, even when commanded by Protestants, was general to all Englishmen in that epoch, and it was strongest of all among the sons of the Cavaliers, whose manor houses had been stormed by the New Model Army, and who had suffered confiscation and persecution while the land was held down for years by Cromwell's Ironsides. Forty years back, a standing army had destroyed the Church of England on behalf of Geneva, and another might now do a similar service for Rome. A prime article of the Tory creed was that a regular army was a danger to the Constitution, and that the island could be defended by a strong navy and by the Militia of the Counties, officered by the squires and local magnates.

The army that had put down Monmouth's rebellion had already become odious by its conduct to the civilian population, irrespective of politics. The poor red-coats, having no barracks provided for them, were billeted on the people, and not being lawfully subject to court martial, their discipline was inevitably lax. Members came up to Westminster, complaining of "the oppression of the soldiers, free quarters, plunder and some felons."

For all these reasons, therefore, when James demanded of the House of Commons, in November 1685, another large sum of money to keep the army on foot, the Commons declined to walk into the trap. The sense of the House as shown in the debates was that the King ought to disband the army and improve the efficiency of the Militia instead. But James declared that the Militia, though loyal, had proved useless during the late Rebellion and that Monmouth had been defeated by the regulars. "There is nothing," he told the Houses, "but a good force of well-disciplined troops in constant pay, that can defend us from such as, either at home or abroad, are disposed to disturb us." These words of James were true; in face of the new model armies now kept up on the Continent, England required a standing force of her own. The regular troops of France or Holland could have walked over our trainbands raw from the plough and the workshop. Moreover, the Militia could not be sent oversea. In the next reign, not only William but his Whig Ministers were to make the case of the Army against the Militia their own. For by that time, owing to the Revolution, the country was able to maintain a standing army that should be subject to the vote of Parliament and could not therefore be used to establish a royal despotism.

But in the winter of 1685 James was asking the Commons to vote enough money to enable him to maintain an army for his own unrevealed purposes: if he obtained it he would be master of Parliament. Very naturally the Commons refused, the more so as the King angrily declined their request that he would, now the Rebellion was over, dispense with the services of the many Roman Catholics to whom he had illegally given commissions. There lay the connection between the question of the Test Act and the question of the standing army; it was on that double issue that the Tory majority in this most loyalist of Parliaments, reluctantly, and in the most courteous language, refused to obey the King. The placemen were not enough to outvote the Tories. Indeed, many even of the placemen voted against the Court and were dismissed. If James wanted the Test Act repealed, he must dissolve this Parliament and remodel the Constituencies over again.

The refusal of the Tory Parliament to repeal the Test Act excluding Roman Catholics from office was the true beginning of the sequence of events that led to the Revolution. The motives of the members who made this vital decision must be studied and understood. It is sometimes argued that because the Test Act, so far as it referred to Roman Catholics, was repealed without evil consequences in 1829, that therefore Parliament did wrong in refusing to repeal it in 1685. But the circumstances were utterly different. The repeal of the Test Act in Hanoverian times, under Protestant Kings controlled by Protestant Parliaments, meant that Roman Catholics would be admitted to the public service in proportion to their merits and their numbers, and with no ulterior end in view save justice between man and man. But in 1685 a zealous and most imprudent Romanist was King, and as the custom of the Constitution then stood, Parliament had neither directly nor indirectly any control over his appointments to the Cabinet, the Privy Council, the Army, the Navy, the Civil Service from the Chief of the Treasury down to the meanest servant in the Custom House, the Bench of Judges, and last but not least the Bench of Bishops. By the winter of 1685 Parliament had grave reason to suspect the truth, that James intended to put Roman Catholics into all the key-places of power in order to Romanize the country. The road to royal favour in all these branches of the Government and public service was to be Roman Catholicism, that is to say for Protestants apostasy. Such was, in fact, the policy followed by James from 1686 to 1688, although the Test Act was not repealed and his action in appointing Roman Catholics to office continued therefore to be illegal. Would he have acted more moderately if Parliament had made it legal for him to appoint his co-religionists? It is absurd to suppose so, and the action of the Tory members in refusing to repeal the Test Act in 1685 was no less fully justified than its repeal under totally different circumstances in 1829.

If James had only sought religious toleration for Roman Catholics he could have had it. In fact, the odious Penal Laws that punished

their religious rites and subjected their priests to death or imprison-
ment had often been suspended in practice, and had been inoperative
during the last years of Charles II. No one for a moment expected
James to renew the persecution of his own religion. Roman Catholics
were, in effect, enjoying freedom of worship, though not by law. If
in 1685 James had asked Parliament to regularize the position by
modifying or repealing the Penal Laws he could certainly have obtained his end. Rochester, Halifax, the Commons themselves had
thrown out feelers in that direction. Such was the advice of the wise
Pope Innocent XI, and such the wish of the old Catholic families of
England, the most loyal and long suffering of all the supporters of
the House of Stuart, who by long and bitter experience knew the
strength of Protestant prejudice among their countrymen. Their prudent request for toleration not ascendancy, was voiced at Court by
their leaders, Lord Powys and Lord Bellasyse.

Already in November 1685 the moderate Catholics, at home and
abroad, feared the consequences of the King's headlong policy, when
he asked Parliament not for the repeal of the Penal Laws but for
the repeal of the Test Act. But instead of listening to the Pope and
the old Catholic families, James listened to the Jesuits and to the
French Ambassador, Barillon; instead of asking Parliament for religious toleration for his co-religionists, he asked for their political
equality, with the set design so to use it as to bring about their
political ascendancy.

Finding that the Commons would neither vote him the large sums
he asked to maintain the Army, nor consent to repeal the Test Act,
James prorogued in anger the most loyalist Parliament that ever was
chosen to support the House of Stuart. It never met again. The memorable session had lasted from November 9 to November 20. Those
eleven days had sufficed to prove that the King's Romanizing policy
would be steadily opposed by Parliament, by the Tories and by the
Anglican Church. The King's first plan for attaining his ends by
law had proved impossible. What would he do next? Would he compromise, as he was besought to do by his daughters who were to
succeed him, by the Pope, by Spain and the Emperor, by the old
English Catholics, not to mention the whole Anglican Church? Or
would he drive straight on over all law, regardless of all opinion,
as the Jesuits and the French Ambassador urged, backed by a few
English time-servers like Jeffreys and Sunderland? At this juncture
the fatal obstinacy of his character decided the future of Britain and

of Europe. He had persuaded himself that his father Charles I had
fallen by making concessions: he would never, he declared, repeat
that mistake. He was so constituted that he could not take unpleasant
advice from his best friends. One of the most loyal of his supporters,
Roger North, wrote of him too truly:

So strong were his prejudices, and so feeble his genius, that he took
none to have any understanding that were not in his measures, and that
the counsel given him to the contrary was for policy of party more than
for friendship for him.

Such a nature was made to be the prey of flatterers. The astute
and unprincipled Sunderland, who in the days of the Popish Plot
had posed as a violent Whig and Exclusionist, saw that he could out-
strip all rivals in the race for power and wealth if he always advised James to follow the inclination of the moment. What would be
the end of it all, this clever but short-sighted gambler never seems
to have asked himself till too late. Sunderland made common cause
with the ambitious fanatic, Father Petre, to encourage every dangerous fancy of the King, and so to get rid of all more timid or
conscientious rivals. Sunderland was soon spoken of as "Premier
Minister." Lord Chancellor Jeffreys, though he sometimes regretted
the King's dangerous and illegal measures, consented to be their instrument, and so saved his place. But Rochester and Clarendon, the
Hyde brothers who represented the extreme High Anglican Toryism,
after making many ignominious concessions to keep office, were
turned out at the New Year 1686-7, because they would not, like
the freethinker Sunderland, pretend to adopt the religion of Rome.
With their fall, the Church of England lost its last real representation at Court. But long ere the Hydes quitted office, the attack on the
Church had begun in earnest.

Since Parliament would not alter the laws, James could only attain
his ends by regarding no law as a restriction on the royal will. The
Prerogative of the Kings of England, their ancient claim to an un-
defined residuary power, had sometimes in the course of our history
swelled to monstrous proportions, and sometimes shrunk back to
little, but never quite to nothing. Prerogative was now to be con-
jured up once more and fashioned into the one substantial reality of
a new English Constitution. This vital change in the royal authority
must be effected by pronouncements from the judicial Bench. James

had already made Jeffreys Lord Chancellor; he could dismiss any Judge who refused to interpret the Prerogative as he wished; he could appoint judges who would act, not as umpires between King and subject, but, in Bacon's phrase, as "lions under the throne." With their help, he might presently be able to manipulate the corporations, magistrates and constituencies, and so nominate a House of Commons as freely as he now nominated the Bench of Judges. Lords he could create in any number, as soon as a new House of Commons had been packed. A Parliament so composed could then alter the laws, and he himself could re-enter on a legal course, when the laws and the Parliament had become mere instruments of the royal will.

James, in short, in his desire to restore Romanism in England, found it necessary to become an absolute monarch like the other Princes of Europe. The absurd mediæval shackles on the royal power, peculiar to our retrograde island, must be removed. Such a policy identified the cause of Roman Catholicism with the cause of despotism in the eyes of a people violently prejudiced against both; it was an alliance that proved ruinous alike to Romanism and to kingly power in England.

Yet James, though he was most imprudent in making such an attempt, had at least some reason to hope for success. He had complete control of the executive power; he could dismiss and nominate every servant of the State, and the higher Church patronage was in his hand. Above all, he had a large army, such as neither the Tudors nor his father or brother had ever commanded in time of peace, and he could replenish it with Catholics from his stronghold in Ireland. In fact, he so far succeeded that his subjects only got the better of him by calling in foreign arms to their aid. Nor even so would he have failed if the Tories and Churchmen had adhered, as he confidently expected them to adhere, to their peculiar doctrine that no one might actively resist the King, even if he broke all the laws and persecuted the Church like Nero. James's other miscalculation was his belief that he could obtain active help from the Puritan Nonconformists, if he relieved them from the operation of the persecuting laws.

The King, moreover, was misled by analogies in contemporary Europe, which did not really apply to England. He saw that the tendency of the age on the Continent was against Protestantism and against popular liberties. The revoker of the Edict of Nantes was the Grand Monarch, feared and admired by all his neighbours. French Protestantism was in its death throes; Dutch, Rhenish and Swiss

Protestants, the neighbours of France, tremblingly awaited their turn. Constitutional liberty was in even worse case. Where were the mediæval Estates of France and Spain? What popular resistance was there to the will of the Princes of Italy and of Germany? Even in stubborn Holland the power of the Stadtholder was on the increase. Poland, indeed, had a free constitution, but its proverbial anarchy was the laughing stock of Europe. Surely, James may well have thought, the tide of a movement so general would float him over the submerged relics of the mediæval Constitution of England. Even the islanders must yield to the modern state necessity for concentrated power.

In one sense James was right: the balance between kingly and parliamentary power in England was continually crippling the efficiency of government, as in this question of a standing army. It must be decided once for all where ultimate power lay. James forced that decision to an issue.

There would, of course, be a difficult time before the King could win through, a hard struggle, and much need for financial economy. So long as that domestic contest continued, all idea of opposing Louis on the Continent must be at an end. As early as October 1685, even before he had quarrelled with Parliament, James had invited the French Ambassador to rejoice with him at the dismissal of their common enemy, Halifax. "I do not think," he said, "the King your Master will be displeased with the removal of Lord Halifax from my counsels. I know, however, the Ministers of the Confederates will be mortified at it." The domestic policy now adopted by James meant reliance on France and breach with his son-in-law William. No Treaty of Alliance was signed with France; none was needed, as Louis himself declared in 1688. James could not oppose Louis, for he had no other friend in Europe; and in England nine-tenths of his subjects were in opposition to his will.

James, by reviving and strengthening Charles II's Anglo-French axis, turned the other powers of Europe, Protestant and Catholic, over to the side of his English enemies. "No Prince," wrote the German historian Ranke, "has ever had less thought for the balance of power in Europe than James II." And "the result was," comments Firth, "that Europe became as indifferent to the fate of James II as James II was to the fate of Europe." At the final crisis William had on his side not only the Protestant Princes of Germany, but Austria, Spain and the Pope himself.

The first round in the struggle for the Prerogative went well for the King. A collusive action was brought against Sir Edward Hales, a Roman Catholic officer whom the King had by letters patent dispensed from the obligation of qualifying as a Protestant under the terms of the Test Act. In June 1686 a Bench of twelve Judges almost unanimously declared that Hales could keep his commission without penalty, because the dispensing power was part of the King's Prerogative, and could be exerted in particular cases for special reasons. It is not possible to condemn this decision as illegal, though it opened a door through which James rushed forward to the wholesale destruction of legal rights. The Kings of England had always possessed, and they still retained after the Revolution, the right to dispense with the operation of a law for special and urgent reasons in some particular case. Such a liberty of executive action is often convenient and sometimes necessary for the public welfare, particularly in commercial matters and especially when Parliament is not in session. If James had merely used this dispensing power, reaffirmed by the Judges in the case of Hales, to retain a few Roman Catholics in his service, little would have been heard of the question. But he proceeded to thrust Roman Catholics wholesale into every branch of the service, civil and military, till finally no Protestant felt safe in his office unless he was prepared to apostatize. And when, by the Declaration of Indulgence, he suspended the entire operation of a whole code of laws, he turned the "dispensing" power, which within strict limits was legal, into a "suspending" power that was utterly illegal and which rendered all law subservient to the mere will of the King.

The more conscientious of the Judges soon began to cry halt to these later developments of the Royal Prerogative. And as fast as they demurred, they were dismissed and replaced by time-servers of paltry pretension as legal authorities. The packing of the Judicial Bench was essential to the successful policy of James. And the independence of Judges was one of the greatest benefits secured at the Revolution.

By packing the Bench, James next obtained a decision on the status of the soldier, that was very necessary to his plans. He depended on the army, which he was gradually handing over to Roman Catholic officers, and into whose ranks he was beginning to introduce batches of Roman Catholic recruits from Ireland. About half the troops were encamped on Blackheath to overawe the Protestant mob of the Capital. The difficulty was to maintain discipline in the ranks. If a private struck his officer he could only be tried for assault before a civil court; if he deserted, he could not be punished more severely than a runaway journeyman. James, by removing recalcitrant Judges like Holt, obtained a decision that desertion was felony, and several deserters were hung in front of their regiments.[1] The King could therefore keep his army together without summoning Parliament. At the Revolution the raising and keeping of a standing army in time of peace without consent of Parliament was declared to have been illegal; and the annual Mutiny Act, passed for one year only, has, ever since 1689, enabled desertion and mutiny to be adequately punished, and discipline to be legally maintained in the army by courts martial, on condition that Parliament meets every year and consents to re-enact the Mutiny Bill and maintain the military forces of the Crown.

James proceeded to break law on law. Prerogative was to be everything, Statutes nothing if they were not to the liking of the King. In 1686 the direct attack on the Church of England was prepared by the revival of the Court of High Commission to govern the Church in virtue of the Royal Supremacy, with the power of suspending and depriving recalcitrant clergymen. This Court was illegal, for it had been abolished by Statute in the first session of Long Parliament in 1641, future Cavaliers and Roundheads voting in full agreement. And the Parliaments of the Restoration had been careful not to restore to the King the power of reviving this Court, for Tories as well as Whigs desired that the Church should hold its freeholds and liberties independent of the Royal will. But in defiance of the Statutes of 1641 and 1661, which expressly prohibited the Crown from setting up Courts with like jurisdiction (*Holdsworth*, VI, pp. 112-18), James revived the Court of High Commission, with Jeffreys as Chief Commissioner, to browbeat and bully bishops, clergymen and dons.

This Court at once proceeded to suspend from his functions Compton, the Bishop of London; his offence had been his refusal illegally to suspend one of his clergy who had defended the doctrine and practice of the Church against those of Rome.

The High Commission was next used in the attack on the Universities, which brought to a head the breach between the King and the

---

[1] The case was not so clear as Macaulay thought, but Holdsworth (*Hist. of English Law*, VI, 228-9) gives fully his reasons for thinking Holt was right, and those Judges wrong who declared desertion to be felony.

old Royalist party. Oxford and Cambridge were the training grounds for the clergy of the Established Church; the King saw that if they could be Romanized, the gradual Romanization of the Established Church would more easily follow. He failed to remember that the Universities, and especially Oxford, were the intellectual and spiritual source of those loyalist and High Tory doctrines to which he had owed his unconditional accession to the throne. If he alienated Oxford, and all men in the country who looked to and loved Oxford, he would cut away the principal prop of his own power.

By a series of arbitrary acts, supported where necessary by the pronouncements of the illegal Court of High Commission, James put three great Oxford Colleges—Christchurch, University and Magdalen—under Romanist rule. Magdalen became a mere Romanist seminary, after its twenty-five Fellows had been illegally ejected from their freehold for their refusal to break the law in the matter of the election of their President.

No action, not even the Trial of the Seven Bishops, did more to alienate the Church. Oxford was the heart of Toryism and Anglicanism and had hitherto been the heart of Royalism. Oxford and the Church had placed James on the throne in spite of the three exclusionist Parliaments—and this was the reward of their loyalty to the House of Stuart and to the person of James. Cambridge, to which he and his family owed far less, came off more lightly; her Vice-Chancellor was merely bullied by Jeffreys and deprived of his office for refusing illegally to admit a Benedictine monk to a degree. But since Christchurch and Magdalen had fallen, it was only a question of time before Trinity and King's would suffer a like fate.

The expulsion of the Fellows of Magdalen was not merely an attack on the Universities, it was by implication an attack on the freehold rights of all ecclesiastical persons. If the clerical Fellows of the famous, beloved and privileged Corporation of Magdalen could not retain their freehold property in face of arbitrary power, still less could simple rectors and vicars when they in their turn should be called on by the High Commission to commit some illegal act. If years were allowed to go by with the King's power thus set high over the laws, the day would come when apostasy or deprivation would be the choice set before all the beneficed clergy of the Established Church. That was why even the High Church Bishops, in spite of their theories of non-resistance, refused to pronounce against rebellion when William landed, and why many of the staunchest

Church laymen actually became rebels. The cause of the King stood in stark opposition to the cause of the law and the cause of the Church.

Early in 1687 it had become clear to James that he could not attain his ends through the assistance of the Anglican Churchmen. He must seek other allies; the handful of half-unwilling Roman Catholics whom he was thrusting into a perilous supremacy could not by themselves govern England; the trickle of conversions to Rome among self-seeking peers, lawyers and place-holders was slow, and years must pass away before Romanists were numerous enough to rule the island alone. Meanwhile, he would rely on the help of the oldest and bitterest enemies of his family and person, the Puritan Nonconformists. They and the Roman Catholics should receive together the same measures of relief from all laws persecuting their worship or excluding them from office, and in return should supply the King with a composite party to override Anglican resistance. Romanists and Roundheads should join in suppressing the Cavaliers.

In accordance with this new policy, James in April 1687 issued his famous Declaration of Indulgence. In the preamble he set forth the blessing of religious toleration, and then proceeded in virtue of his royal prerogative to suspend the Clarendon Code, the Test Act of 1673, and all laws injurious either to Catholic or Protestant Dissenters. Charles II, before the passing of the Test Act, had issued a similar though less extensive Declaration of Indulgence, but had been forced by Parliament to withdraw it as illegal.

The power to "suspend" Statutes wholesale, claimed by James's Declaration, was very different from the power to "dispense" with the action of a Statute in some particular case like that of Hales. The "dispensing power" had been pronounced legal in proper circumstances; but this larger claim to "dispense with laws in a lump," as a Member of Parliament termed it, or the "suspending" power as it was distinctively called, subverted all Constitutional restraints upon the King. It had been pronounced illegal both by Charles II and his Parliament. Indeed, if it was legal, there was no more law save the royal will.

Would the Protestant Dissenters embrace the offer and become the King's allies? They were suffering daily from cruel persecution from which the King gave them immediate though illegal relief. Protected by the Declaration of Indulgence, they resumed their religious serv-

ices openly, and some of the earliest Nonconformist chapels bear the
date 1687. But would they, in gratitude to the King, join with the
Jesuits to set up royal despotism? They might in that way enjoy a
sweet revenge on their Anglican persecutors—but for how long?
Either the King and his religion would grow strong with the passage
of years, till the Jesuits felt strong enough to treat the English Puritans as their co-religionists in France were being treated by James's
friend and patron, or else the King would fail, or possibly die, and
under his Protestant successors, William and Mary, an Anglican
Parliament would meet to take fierce vengeance on all who had attacked the Church and Constitution of England. And, apart from all
such prudent and self-regarding calculations, could the sons of the
Roundheads be so base as to betray the Protestant cause and the
liberties of Parliament?

A minority of Nonconformist leaders consented to become the
King's allies; among these was one excellent man, the Quaker William Penn; but the great majority of the Puritans, including the
leaders of highest moral authority such as Richard Baxter and John
Bunyan, rallied to the national cause. And this rally became more
general and more active as the years 1687 and 1688 went by, and
the fundamentally Romanist and despotic aims of the King became
every week more apparent.

Important pronouncements by interested parties helped to keep the
Puritan sects on the side of the Church and the nation. In the first
place, the bishops and the political chiefs of the Anglican or Tory
party definitely promised to support an Act of Toleration for Puritan worship as soon as a free Parliament should meet—a promise
fulfilled in 1689. In this "strange auction" Church and King bid
against each other for the support of their old enemies, and by the
summer of 1688 the Church had clearly outbidden the King.

In the second place, William of Orange, in the name of himself
and his wife as heir presumptive to the throne, let it be known from
The Hague that he opposed his father-in-law's policy, that he favoured freedom of religious worship for Protestant and for Catholic
Dissenters, but that he deprecated the Repeal of the Test Act and the
admission of Roman Catholics to office. Such was the traditional policy of the House of Orange in Holland—religious freedom but not
political equality for Roman Catholics. Its enunciation by William
as his panacea for England in 1687 pleased Anglican and Puritan,
and was regarded as reasonable by the anti-French party on the

Continent, the Pope, Spain, Austria, and even by the moderate or old Catholic party in England, who looked to William to protect them from the worst reprisals if James should die.

The Puritan Nonconformists had therefore a firm promise of a Toleration Act from the Tory party and from the heirs presumptive to the throne. A secure future was theirs if they would wait, and not betray the Protestant interest in their hurry to enjoy the precarious favour of James. The choice before them was set out in Halifax's famous "Letter to a Dissenter." In this cool and witty analysis of the situation, the Trimmer put before the Puritans the danger of alliance with the Jesuits, and the need for national solidarity against James. The "Letter" was anonymous and was at first issued in August 1687 by a secret press, as was most of the anti-Government literature of the reign.[1] The Censorship could prevent open publication, but its net could not stem the tide of pamphlets from Holland and from the secret presses of London. The "Letter to a Dissenter" had an immense circulation and a great influence at a critical juncture.

Consider, [wrote Halifax to the Dissenters] that these new friends did not make you their choice but their refuge. . . . There must be something extraordinary when the Church of Rome setteth up bills [advertisements, like a quack doctor's] and offereth plaisters for tender consciences; by all that hath hitherto appeared her skill in chirurgery lyeth chiefly in a quick hand, to cut off limbs. . . . Think a little how dangerous it is to build on a foundation of paradoxes. Popery is now the only friend to liberty; and the known enemy to persecution. . . . Things tend naturally to what you would have if you would let them alone, and not by an unseasonable activity lose the influences of your good star that promiseth you everything that is prosperous. The Church of England, convinced of its error in being severe to you; the Parliament, whenever it meeteth, sure to be gentle to you; the next heir bred in the country which you have so often quoted for a pattern of indulgence [Holland]; a general agreement of all thinking men that one must no longer cut ourselves off from the Protestants abroad, but rather enlarge the foundations upon which we are to build our defences against the common enemy, so that in truth all things conspire to give you ease and satisfaction, if by too much haste to anticipate your good fortune you do not destroy it.

In the summer of 1687 James was encouraged to hope for the

[1] "There was a pamphlet entitled 'A Letter to a Dissenter' went about in the dark and sold very deare, which was answered by Sir Robert (Roger) Lestrange; and both being now printed, are publicly sold for 6d., so much benefit the world hath by Sir Robert his answer." (*Bramston Autobiography*, p. 300.)

Nonconformist alliance by a number of addresses of thanks from various dissenting communities up and down the country, whom the Declaration of Indulgence had relieved from actual persecution. Thinking that he had the Puritans with him, he proceeded to remodel the county magistracy, the Corporations that governed the towns and the bodies that elected the Members of Parliament, turning out the Tories who for half a dozen years past had enjoyed almost a monopoly of these strategical positions in the body politic. He replaced them with Roman Catholic gentlemen of old family, many of them unwilling conscripts to a policy they knew to be imprudent, cheek by jowl with dissenting merchants and shopkeepers of the old Roundhead and Shaftesbury tradition in politics. The Whig lords and squires either were not offered or did not accept any share in the royal favours, but some of the rank and file of the broken Whig party, of the Nonconformist middle-class, took offices which they were not entitled by law to hold, and thus enrolled themselves as partisans of the King and the Declaration of Indulgence.

In the last years of Charles II the time-honoured charters of London and many other towns had been cancelled by *quo warranto* proceedings of doubtful legality, or had been surrendered under pressure to avoid penalties. New charters had been granted by the King's Prerogative, giving a monopoly of the new Corporations to Tory partisans. The Tories had rejoiced in this doubtful exercise of royal power by Charles II, since it had been used to place them in the seats of their enemies. But they came quickly to reconsider the question of royal prerogative in relation to municipal liberties, when James II repeated the action of his brother, in order to turn out Tories and Anglicans wholesale from the Corporations, and substitute Roman Catholics and Puritans.

The shattering effect upon Tory loyalty that resulted from James II's purge of the Town Corporations and the rural magistracy can be illustrated in the words of the Earl of Aylesbury, the highest of Tories, who eventually became a Jacobite and went into exile from a touching personal loyalty to a master whose policy he had so strongly disapproved:

In pursuing the two lamentable and unadvised steps—the seizing of St. Mary Magdalen College and the imprisoning and trial of the Bishops, I omitted one thing that was greatly prejudicial to the King, and that was the purging of the Corporations great and small, expelling all loyal and good subjects, and that were entirely in his Majesty's interest, and in the worst of time when he was Duke of York, and after when he came to the Crown. . . .

The City of London was the chief sacrifice, and no doubt but in the annals you will find the names of those unparalleled magistrates turned out . . . those two pillars of Church and Monarchy, Sir John Moore and Sir William Pritchard, who was the author of the overthrow of factious and seditious riots, and was the cause of the flight into Holland of that turbulent Earl [Shaftesbury] who died there soon after. There were seven or eight more turned out, and the same number restored or made anew, and all of the fanatic spawn. . . . [On the occasion of the King's visit to the City.] I took notice to a Lord in my coach what sneaking faces most of the livery-men of the Companies had, that lined the streets. 'Can you wonder at it?' said that Lord, 'all the jolly, genteel citizens are turned out and all sneaking fanatics put into their places.'

In short, enough "fanatics," as the Tories called all Puritans, had joined the King's party to encourage him in his course and to enrage the most loyal Tories against him; but these time-serving politicians who now as "King's men" filled the Town Corporations, were not strong enough in numbers or in character to have any considerable influence. And as the fateful months went by, the Puritan bodies throughout the country turned more and more against the King. In relying upon the Puritans, James leaned on a staff that broke in his hands.

The efforts of James throughout the greater part of 1687 and 1688 were directed to packing a new House of Commons that would support his policy and repeal the Test Act. The remodelling of the Corporations was partly directed to this end; the remodelling of the county magistracy on similar lines was no less essential and proved even more difficult. In the towns James could at least find a certain amount of precarious support from a minority of the Puritan merchants. In the country districts he could find few country gentlemen to serve him apart from the Roman Catholics, many of whom came in as "pressed men" disliking the whole business. Among the Protestants, the Tory and the Whig country gentlemen were equally opposed to the royal policy. In order to enjoy the royal favour, country gentlemen were asked whether they would support the repeal of the Test Act if elected as members of the new Parliament, or whether they would support candidates so pledged. The King's busy agents went round the country houses canvassing the squires individually on these lines, using at once threats and promises, but almost always without avail.[1] The similarity of the answers returned to the royal questionnaire show that there must have been much secret consultation among the Whig and Tory gentlemen in all the counties of England. The united party that made the Revolution was beginning to take form, though as yet only for the purpose of passive resistance.

James found that he was unable to pack a Parliament for his purposes, though he tried harder than any King of England had ever tried before. Therefore, after he had dissolved his old Tory Parliament, he never in fact summoned another, though he never wholly abandoned the idea. But he dismissed the Tory Lords Lieutenant, Deputy Lieutenants and Justices of the Peace by whom the counties were governed, putting in their place Roman Catholics and Puritans who had less than no influence, and some of whom were at heart opposed to his policy. The complete collapse of the royal power in county after county when William landed was due to the fact that the King had no effective local magistracy at his command. If the King had had a paid bureaucracy of his own in the counties, like the King of France in his provinces, he might have pulled through. But he depended on the loyalty of an unpaid magistracy composed of independent country gentlemen. It was an instrument that could only be used for policies not wholly repugnant to the class from which it was drawn.

The office of Justice of the Peace had been established in Plantagenet times as a working compromise between the powers claimed by the Crown and the influence exercised by local landowners. The Tudor and Stuart monarchs had for 200 years tried to make these unpaid local magistrates subserve the purposes of a bureaucracy devoted to the partisan projects of the Crown. The Tudors had succeeded well enough because a large section of the country gentlemen favoured their Reformation policy. The earlier Stuarts had succeeded rather less well, but James II failed altogether, because he asked the country gentlemen to help him in a policy which nine-tenths of them abhorred, and which was equally abhorred by the other classes of the community.

[1] See Sir George Duckett's *Penal Laws and Test Act returns,* 1882–3; see also the most interesting diary of Sir John Knatchbull, published in the *Cambridge Historical Journal* for 1926 by P. C. Vellacott, sometime Head Master of Harrow.

In one aspect, therefore, the Revolution was a revolt of the local magistracy against the Central Power. The revolt was necessary to save the Constitutional liberties of England. But it was unfortunate that the independence of the local magistrates was increased by the events of 1688-9—as it most certainly was—for what England needed in the interest of good government and social reform was not less central control but more. James, however, had identified the cause of central control with Roman Catholicism and lawless despotism. In the reaction that followed, central control lost yet more ground. Throughout the eighteenth century the local magistracies in town and county did only too much what they liked, without any restraint by King or Privy Council. It was only the rise of democracy and Benthamite Reform in the nineteenth century that re-adjusted the balance between Whitehall and the local magistrates.

Already in the early months of 1688, the union of classes, parties and churches against the King and his Jesuit advisers was obliterating all old landmarks and superseding the feuds of Whig and Tory, Church and Dissent. These old enemies, and the great middle mass of opinion not permanently attached to either faction, now formed a solid phalanx in defence of the Constitution and the Protestant religion of England. As much as any political movement recorded in our annals, it was a moral revival. And certainly a moral revival was overdue. By reaction from the shibboleths and the hypocrisy of the Puritan regime, the reign of Charles II had been a period of lax political morality, and scepticism as to the reality of virtue. The political classes had made a jest of principle. Men like Buckingham, Shaftesbury and Sunderland had been characteristic leaders of that scapegrace epoch. James, having watched the conduct of public men throughout his brother's reign, had been led to hope that there was no religious conviction or moral feeling in England sufficient to resist the force of royal displeasure and royal favour, if steadily exercised to make men change their religion. The challenge was an insult to the nation, but not wholly undeserved. It evoked a memorable response. The Tory pamphleteer Davenant, a dozen years later, recalled how these times had stirred men's souls:

The measures King James the Second took to change the religion of the country, roused up fresh zeal in the minds of all sorts of men: they embraced more straitly what they were in fear to lose. Courtiers did thrust themselves into the presence to quit their offices rather than be brought to do what might prejudice the Church of England. Nor had the licentious ways of living in fleets and armies shaken our seamen and soldiers in their principles. They all stood firm. The clergy showed themselves prepared to die with their flocks, and managed the controversial parts of Divinity with primitive courage and admirable learning. The churches were everywhere crowded, and the prospect of persecution, though peradventure at some distance, begot devotion.

And if principle was enlisted against James so too was prejudice. The violent anticlerical passions of the English mob, easily aroused to burn the chapels of Puritan dissenters, regarded Jesuits and the Roman worship with even more furious hatred and fear. The political temperature of English opinion in the summer of 1688 would certainly have sufficed to restrain either Charles I or Charles II. But James, obstinate in the belief that his father had fallen because he made concessions, and himself surrounded by flatterers who deceived him in order to cling to their offices, not only held his course but flung into the loaded mine the lighted match of the Trial of the Seven Bishops.

The famous trial arose out of the republication, in the spring of 1688, of the Declaration of Indulgence, issued the year before. There was little change in the substance of the Declaration; again "stacks of statutes" were swept into the dustbin by royal decree. But on this occasion a further step was taken. The clergy of the Establishment were required by the King to read the Declaration in their churches after the morning service. There were few beneficed clergymen in England who did not believe the Declaration to be illegal; yet they were one and all to be made partners in the illegality. Any parson who refused, was liable to be brought up before the High Commission Court and suspended or deprived for disobedience. The Church had to bethink herself what policy to adopt in this desperate strait. If indeed the whole body of clergy refused to read the Declaration, it would certainly be difficult, perhaps impossible, to proceed against them. But could such unanimity be hoped for? And if some read and others did not, the disobedient might be victimized. A common policy was required. Obedience to the King had long been the chief doctrine taught by the Church of England; what, if any, were the limits to obedience?

After anxious debates with the ecclesiastical and lay leaders of the

Church party, Archbishop Sancroft and the majority of his suffragans recommended universal disobedience to the King's order.

The significance of the Primate's advice to his clergy [1] was all the greater because Sancroft was by nature a shy and retiring man, and belonged to the strictest school of High Churchmen, who had hitherto taught that the King's will was the guide for all true subjects and Christians. Up till now, Sancroft had been hesitating and backward in resistance to James, much as he regretted his policy; but at his supreme crisis he did not hesitate. He and his leading suffragans now declared that Parliament and not the King was the source of law, and that the King out of Parliament could not suspend Statutes. The Declaration therefore, in the eyes even of these High Tories, was illegal, and they advised the clergy to refuse to read it. But they reiterated their promise to support an Act of Toleration for Dissenting worship when Parliament should meet. The Church and Tory party had ceased to be an ultra-Royalist and had again become a parliamentary party, and it now stood pledged to Religious Toleration, which had hitherto been advocated only by the Whigs. Here lay the embryo of the Revolution Settlement.

On the Sunday when the London clergy had been commanded to read the Declaration, only four out of a hundred obeyed.

They had been encouraged in this refusal by the leading Dissenters in London, who declared they did not wish for relief by means of the Declaration, which would destroy the laws and the Protestant religion. A fortnight later the clergy throughout the rest of the country were called on to read the Declaration, and followed the example set by London. The Church had defied the King.

In face of opposition from such a quarter, and indeed from almost every quarter, James might well have receded. Instead he went forward to put Sancroft and six other Bishops on trial for seditious libel—for so he designated the petition they had presented to him begging that the clergy should not be forced to read the Declaration because it was illegal. Even Sunderland, who had 60,000 livres a year from France and had just gone through the form of reconciliation to Rome in order to keep his place at the head of the Government, was aghast at the audacity, and began to fear that he as well as his master had gone too far. He unwillingly signed the committal

[1] There was at the moment no Archbishop of York.

of the Seven Bishops, but he began a policy of "insurance" by communicating secretly with William of Orange.

The Trial of the Seven Bishops, the greatest historical drama that ever took place before an authorized English law court, aroused popular feeling to its height. The sight of seven prelates of blameless character and known loyalty to James (five of them were afterwards Jacobites!) entering the Tower as prisoners and standing in the dock as culprits, showed as nothing else would have done that the most revered and the most loyal subjects in the land would be broken if they refused to become active parties to the King's illegal designs. If the Bishops suffered, who could hope to escape the royal vengeance?

The accused had the advantage of the fact that it was a public trial. On June 29, 1688, Westminster Hall and the streets and open places around it were thronged by a vast multitude, all swayed by one intense emotion. Nearly half the House of Lords came as spectators of the drama; the leading public men in the country filled the court of King's Bench, to see the Bishops get fair play. The Judges had by this time been well weeded by the King, but on this occasion two out of four ventured to advise the jury in favour of the accused—a piece of independence for which next week they were both dismissed. An attempt by the prisoners' counsel to obtain an acquittal on technicalities failed, and the issues left to the jury were therefore the real issues of the case: Had subjects the right to petition the monarch, and was the Declaration of Indulgence illegal? The jury, held up all night by a single dissentient, came next day to a unanimous verdict of Not Guilty. The scene in court after the acquittal, the day of furious joy in the streets of the capital, followed by the night of bonfires and of windows each illuminated with seven candles, the yet more ominous cheering of the King's own troops on Hounslow Heath, would have warned anyone but James that the ground was cracking under his feet.

But he would not recede. A new hope lured him on; he had a new motive for persistence. Nearly three weeks before the trial of the Bishops, the Queen (his second wife Mary of Modena), had borne him a son. She had so long been childless that people were astounded at a natural fact that touched their interests so nearly. "In the seventeenth century people would believe anything. The Catholics thought it was a miracle, and the Protestants said it was an imposture. It was neither." (G. N. Clark, p. 121. See below, p. 248.)

The unfortunate little Prince, destined in after years to be known as "James III" or the "Old Pretender," was, of course, James II's son. But his father had been unwise in not summoning more Protestant witnesses among the crowd that, according to custom, witnessed the birth of the heir to the throne. The story that the infant had been introduced into the Queen's bed in a warming-pan or otherwise, was exploited by the enemies of James, working on a nation that believed the Jesuits capable of any villainy. Anne for long honestly doubted whether the young James were her brother or not. And the Tories generally found relief for conscience in the doubt. The Whigs cared less about it, and after using it in 1688, soon let it drop, because they did not believe in divine right and were quite pleased to exclude the Prince even if he were the King's son. Indeed, the Tories in later years upbraided the Whigs for repudiating the warming-pan story at the Sacheverell Trial, and in 1711 Swift wrote in the Tory *Examiner* that the popular belief ought to be maintained "whether it be true or false."

In June 1688 the birth of the Prince made the quarrel between the King and the nation far more serious and irreconcilable. There was now an heir apparent to the throne, a boy who would by right displace the presumptive Protestant heirs, his half-sisters Mary and Anne. And no one could doubt that his Roman Catholic parents would bring him up in their own faith. Hitherto many Tories had been prepared to wait patiently for relief till the death of James, when all his plans would fall to the ground on the succession of his Protestant daughters. But now a long line of Roman Catholic Kings would carry on his policy, unless his subjects resorted to armed resistance.

While the birth of the Prince thus moved the minds of Whig and Tory leaders to plot the Revolution, it gave James a new reason to be obstinate in his course. If he could live till the child was of age, all would be well; and if, as was not unlikely, he died while his son was still a child, he must leave behind him a Roman Catholic party in such power that the Protestants would be prevented from getting hold of little James and bringing him up in the religion of the Church of England. Thus the Trial of the Seven Bishops and the birth of the Prince of Wales together ushered in the revolutionary period of James's reign. The historian must now dive into the annals of conspiracy and weigh the prospects of revolt.

IV   THE REVOLUTION

On June 30, 1688, the day of the acquittal of the Seven Bishops, a document was secretly dispatched to William of Orange, inviting him to come over to England with a military force, round which the country would rally in rebellion against the government of James. There was no offer of the Crown or any indication as to what the ultimate settlement should be. The invitation was signed in cypher by Devonshire, Russell and Sidney for the Whigs, by Danby and the Bishop of London for the Church and Tory party, and by Shrewsbury and Lumley, whose signatures attested the renewed zeal of the nation for Protestantism, to which both those noblemen had recently become converts.

For a year or more past, the Whig and Tory leaders, forgetful of old feuds, had been consulting secretly for the defence of the public rights, often in concert with Dykvelt, the trusted agent of William, representing his wife Mary the heir presumptive to the throne. The plans of constitutional resistance that had been generally adopted throughout the country had been matured in such conferences, but until the spring of 1688 the idea of an armed rising had not been considered either in London or at The Hague. Then the pace quickened, and in June the trial of the Seven Bishops, and still more the birth of the Prince of Wales, persuaded the bolder spirits among the two English parties that resort must be had to force.

It was not too soon, for the feeling against James could not become stronger or more universal than it was already. And next year might be too late, for popular ferment is subject to periods of ebb through sheer exhaustion. Moreover, James had begun to transform his army by the introduction of recruits from Catholic Ireland. This process was deeply resented by the English soldiers, who regarded the Irish as an inferior and conquered race, and were themselves more than ever estranged from the King. The redcoats encamped on Hounslow Heath had cheered the news of the Bishops' acquittal. If indeed James were allowed time to introduce enough Irish, he might again trust to the loyalty of his regiments; but meanwhile the morale of his army was in dire confusion. He was swapping horses in midstream, and the Revolution was deliberately timed to catch him in the act.

Except by rebellion there was no longer hope of relief. Even if people continued to regard the Prince of Wales as supposititious, he would succeed to the throne if James died in possession of power. Constitutional resistance had reached the limit of its efficacy. The Bishops might be acquitted, but all executive authority remained in the King's hands. He was busy remodelling the Army, the Judiciary, the Magistracy, the Parliamentary Constituencies. How long was it safe to allow him a free hand? For though James had law against him, he had power on his side, and if once he could pack a House of Commons, as he was diligently striving to do, Parliament would put him right with the law, for new Statutes could transform it into a law of absolutism. These reasons for immediate action were clearly set before William in the Invitation of June 30.

Whig doctrine of a contract between King and people justified rebellion against a law-breaking King; and half the Tories, headed by their old leader Danby and by Compton, Bishop of London, had now been converted to Whig doctrine on that point. The other half of the Tories, headed by Archbishop Sancroft and Lord Nottingham would not indeed join in rebellion, but would at least refrain from defending the King by word or deed, until his power to do harm had been destroyed by others less scrupulous than themselves. For the doctrine of non-resistance demanded only passive, not active, obedience to a tyrannical King. According to the High Church divines, St. Paul had taught that the Christians should submit to Nero, but not that they should fly to arms to defend their persecutor against a conspiracy of the Pretorian Guard. The enemies of James, therefore, calculated that the King's power would fall, because all the Whigs and half the Tories would be active in rebellion, while the other half of the Tories looked on with folded arms.

Indeed, the only real danger to the initial success of a revolt lay

in the armed forces of the Crown. To meet this, a conspiracy, cen-
tring on Lord Churchill (afterwards the great Marlborough), was
widely spread among the army officers; other agents were busy
among the Captains of the Navy. The rank and file of the regiments,
and the deck hands, though not in the conspiracy, were deeply
alienated from James—whether to the point of mutiny no one could
tell until the day. The Navy was thought to be even more zealously
Protestant than the Army, and moreover in those days of sailing
ships a "Protestant wind" might give the invader an undisturbed
landing, as indeed happened. But it was agreed that a considerable
armed force must be brought into England by any would-be Liber-
ator, not necessarily large enough to defeat the King's regiments in
battle, for it was earnestly hoped to avoid a conflict—but enough to
hold them in check by manœuvre till they had disintegrated through
disaffection and desertion, and till the rest of the country had risen
in arms. If the flag of rebellion were raised without serious military
support, as Monmouth had rashly raised it, few would dare to join;
Sedgemoor and the Bloody Assize were fresh in recollection.

It is often asked: Why did the Whigs and Tories of 1688 call in
foreign arms? Why did they not rise in rebellion as Englishmen in
their own quarrel, like the Roundheads of 1642? They had a better
case, and the country was far more united against James II than
against Charles I. Why then invite foreigners to interfere? The fact
that James was introducing Irish, whom the English regarded as
foreigners more odious than the Dutch, is an excuse, but not in itself
an answer.

The answer lies in the difference of the situation. In 1642 Charles I
had no army save what he could raise from loyalist volunteers; in
1688 James had a large regular army on foot. In 1642 a Parliament
was sitting as a centre of authority round which men could rally
against the King; in 1688 no Parliament was sitting. A flag or leader
was therefore needed to evoke and organize opposition to James.

There must then be an army of liberation, and there must also be
a chieftain under whose banner all sections of the opposition would
gladly march. The only army available for such a purpose would
be a large draft from the professional troops of the Dutch Republic
—a polyglot Protestant force, including a British contingent whose
presence would go far to mitigate the sense of a foreign invasion.
And the only person round whom Whigs and Tories would rally
with equal confidence was William of Orange, husband of the King's

eldest child Mary. By a happy coincidence William as Stadtholder of Holland was the one man who could bring over the desired force. He could also, as head of the European combination in restraint of France, enlist as supporters of his expedition against the ally of Louis XIV, not only the Protestant Princes of Germany, but Spain, Austria and, strangest of all, the Pope himself!

For reasons connected chiefly with the later years of his reign in England, William III is usually remembered as a Whig, rather than as a Tory hero. But in 1688 and for several years after the Revolution he appeared as a leader equally agreeable and disagreeable to both parties, and his own feelings were not more Whig than Tory.

In religion, indeed, he pleased the Whigs best, for he was a latitudinarian Calvinist, prepared to conform to the Church of England. He was by temper, conviction and policy in favour of religious toleration (even to Roman Catholics), and he was above all for the hearty union of all Protestants, in face of the power of Louis that had just destroyed them in France and was threatening them in Holland and on the Rhine. William was, in short, what our ancestors called a "low churchman." This the Tories could tolerate but not applaud; it pleased the Whigs well.

On the other hand William's political connections were more Tory than Whig. His oldest English champion was the Tory leader Danby, who had negotiated his marriage with Mary in 1677, and the Tories had protected their reversionary claims to the throne, when the more violent of the Whigs were trying to supplant them both by Monmouth, a wrong that William could not quickly forgive. Moreover, he represented in his own person the anti-Republican party in Holland. As Dutch Stadtholder and as head of a princely house, he held views of royal prerogative which were rather Tory than Whig. He suspected the Whigs as crypto-Republicans, jealous of the royal power which he secretly hoped to obtain in order to use it for the defeat of Louis of France. For that purpose he coveted as much authority in England as he could get. If he could become King, he wished for kingly power. Although, unlike James, he was prepared to observe all laws limiting royal prerogative, he had no wish to see his class of law increased. He was himself a grandson of Charles I; the House of Orange and its partisans had been bitterly hostile to the rebels who cut off his head. William, in short, was no Whig, and in 1688 he was about equally in favour with both the English parties, whose factious quarrels he understood, regretted and despised. He regarded the misconduct of Whigs and Tories for a number of years as a chief cause of the French danger in Europe, and of the domestic troubles that now justly afflicted the English themselves.

William did not come over for love of England or for pity of her misfortunes. Neither the country nor its inhabitants made any appeal to his affections, which were all centred on Holland. His wife loved England, but he was not in the habit of forming his policy in consultation with Mary, nor would she have urged him to attack her own father. Her gentle nature felt the whole tragedy of her position, but she silently accepted the decision of the husband she adored, as to the only means of saving England, Holland and the Protestant cause in Europe.

William, then, was under no personal or moral obligation to risk the fortunes of the little land of dykes and canals for the sake of a country that had often treated both him and Holland very ill. But in his cold judgment, Holland could only be saved from ultimate conquest by France, if England was brought in as an active partner of the anti-French alliance which he had painfully built up in Europe. If he could himself become King of England that object would certainly be secured. Failing that, the object might still be attained if the policy of James were subjected to the will of a freely elected Parliament. For that reason he decided that the enormous risks of the invasion of England must be faced, and he proceeded to make his preparations—military, diplomatic and political—with a combined audacity and wisdom that mark him out as one of the world's great men.

William's Declaration, with which he heralded his coming, announced that he had been invited by certain Lords Spiritual and Temporal to restore the ravished liberties of the English people. The essential clause of the Declaration was that which appealed to a freely elected Parliament to decide on all questions at issue. "A free Parliament" was the very same cry which Monk had raised as the prelude to the restoration of Charles II. There were indeed many similarities in the movements of 1660 and 1688. In both cases the object was to get rid of arbitrary and lawless power supported by military force, to restore the ancient laws and the authority of a freely elected Parliament. And in both cases these ends were found to be best secured and perpetuated by placing a new King upon the throne.

William and the Englishmen who invited him over clearly saw

that an appeal to a free Parliament was the only possible cry which would unite all the enemies of James, Whig and Tory, Church and Dissent. Any premature indication of the nature of the Settlement that was to follow the revolt, above all any hint that James was to be dethroned, or on the other hand, that he was to be kept on the throne, would divide the nation at the very moment when union was essential. It would arouse debate when swift action was wanted. It was enough to announce that a free Parliament should decide all matters in dispute. But a Parliament could not be freely elected, and if elected could not have power to decide these tremendous issues, unless the military power of James had first been broken. What his position would be after he had been disarmed would depend partly on Parliament, and even more perhaps upon himself.

The political and diplomatic difficulties that William had to overcome before he could set sail were so great that even his ability would not have sufficed without a rare run of luck.

The Dutch were not a venturesome people and their unanimous consent had to be obtained for this very risky adventure. The Republican party that dominated the great City of Amsterdam wished to limit the Stadtholder's power, and would in normal times have been most unwilling to see William strengthen his position in Holland by becoming King of England. Moreover, the Republican party was the Peace party, anxious to remain on good terms with France, and if the Dutch attacked James they would certainly find themselves at war with his protector Louis XIV. The party hostile to William formed, indeed, only a minority in the Dutch States-General, but the Federal Constitution of the United Provinces enabled even a very small minority to hold up decisive action. Any one of the Seven Provinces, and any one City in any of those Provinces, had the right to veto the use of the Army and Fleet of the Federation on the projected expedition. All William's statecraft could not have obtained the required unanimity, if his enemy Louis XIV had not played into his hands.

If in 1688 Louis had either spoken the Dutch Republic fair, or if he had kept a large army near her frontier, in either case William would never have obtained leave to sail. But the French King was in one of his outrageous moods, which on several occasions in his life undid the work of years of policy. In 1688 he insulted and bullied the Dutch till even the Republican Peace party rallied to William.

And at the same time he withdrew the forces that threatened Holland, to plunge them into a campaign against the German Princes on the Rhine. The Dutch came to the unanimous conclusion that they must seize the fleeting moment of safety created by the removal of the French armies to the Rhine, and send their Stadtholder to win the alliance of England, because nothing else would render them ultimately secure from so bad a neighbour as Louis. And thus at the last moment they gave William leave to go, taking with him the Dutch Fleet and many regiments in the Dutch service.

Why did Louis make the greatest mistake of his life in withdrawing military pressure from Holland in the summer of 1688? He was vexed with James, who unwisely chose this moment of all, to refuse the help and advice of his French patron, upon whose friendship he had based his whole policy. But Louis was not entirely passion's slave. No doubt he felt irritation with James, but he also calculated that, even if William landed in England, there would be civil war and long troubles, as always in that factious island. Meanwhile, he could conquer Europe at leisure. "For twenty years," says Lord Acton, "it had been his desire to neutralize England by internal broils, and he was glad to have the Dutch out of the way [in England] while he dealt a blow at the Emperor Leopold [in Germany]." He thought "it was impossible that the conflict between James and William should not yield him an opportunity." This calculation was not as absurd as it looks after the event. It was only defeated by the unexpected rapidity, peacefulness and solidity of a new type of Revolution. What happened was contrary to all precedent. The revolutionary movement that began in England in 1640, had dragged on for a dozen years before it produced Cromwell in shining armour, prepared to interfere effectively in the affairs of Europe. But the Revolution of 1688 produced, in a few months, a united nation hurling defiance at Louis, and, though not at the moment expert in war, doggedly determined to re-learn that art through years of experience, till Louis was defeated and Europe saved.

By the end of September 1688 it was everywhere known that the preparations in the Dutch dockyards were directed against the English government. James at length took alarm, and offered great concessions to public opinion. He abolished the Court of High Commission, replaced the ejected Fellows of Magdalen, restored the old

Charters to London and other cities, and offered to put back in the Lord-Lieutenancies and on the Bench of Magistrates many of the Tory nobles and gentlemen whom he had removed.

These concessions, made six months earlier, would have had a profound effect. Now they had no effect at all. They were too clearly the result of the impending invasion from Holland. Moreover, even now he refused to give way on the fundamental issue, the Suspending Power. He still kept the Roman Catholics in office, contrary to the law which he still considered he had the right to suspend by his personal fiat. Many, therefore, of those Tories whom he offered to restore to the magistracy refused to act, so long as persons disqualified by law remained as their colleagues on the county Bench, or their official chiefs at Whitehall. Even those who consented to resume their old posts felt no moral obligation to support James against William. In short, the hesitations and changes of the King's policy in October only weakened and confused the position of his servants when the crisis came next month.

The anger and distrust of the country had risen to such a height that it could not be dispelled by partial concessions made under duress, which could be withdrawn when the danger had passed. Too much had been done in the last three years to be forgiven at a word. Old Sir John Bramston blurted out to a royal agent the real feeling of the Tory squires when asked to resume the service of the Crown at the eleventh hour—"Some would think one kick of the breech enough for a gentleman."

The King's subjects did well to be sceptical. James was determined never to be a Constitutional monarch or to abandon his efforts to secure the ultimate ascendancy of his religion. If in October he had really meant to surrender, he would have summoned a freely elected Parliament, as he was besought to do by all who desired reconciliation. He issued writs for an election and withdrew them again on October 28. He had said to the Spanish Ambassador, "I will either win all or lose all," and his subsequent flight to France was only the final proof of his determination not to remain King at the price of abandoning his designs. He was no self-interested schemer; if he had been such, he could have remained on the throne. His firm adherence to principle may perhaps claim our admiration. It may certainly claim our gratitude, for it made the issues clear, and led to a lasting solution.

The fears that brought James himself to partial and tardy concessions, struck terror into time-servers at Court. The arch-hypocrite
Sunderland had turned Roman Catholic in the summer in order to
secure his place against rivals. Scarcely had he burnt his boats in this
fashion, when he began to smell Revolution in the air. To insure his
head and his estates, he began to give moderating advice on the
Council Board, and entered into secret correspondence with William. He fell under suspicion, and James dismissed him from office
at the end of October.

There remained at the King's side the Chancellor Jeffreys and the
Jesuit Petre, the two most unpopular men in the island, who proved
mere chaff before the wind in the storm that was rising. Godolphin,
Dartmouth, Aylesbury and Middleton still continued as faithful servants but not as advisers of the King, whose policy they had long
disapproved. When William landed, James was giving ear to no conservative statesman of the front rank answering to Hyde and Falk-
land, whose wisdom had done so much to guide the counsels and
retrieve the errors of Charles I during the months immediately pre-
ceding the outbreak of the Civil War. James had driven all such into
opposition like Halifax and Nottingham, or into rebellion like Danby.
Nor was there any Prince Rupert to revive the spirit of his army and
lead it to the attack of invaders and rebels. The Commander-in-Chief,
Lord Feversham, was slothful and incompetent; the Lieutenant-
General, Lord Churchill, soon to be proved the greatest soldier of
the age, was at the head of a secret conspiracy among the officers to
save the laws and religion of England. He and his wife, Sarah, had
persuaded their friend, the Princess Anne, James's second child, to
take the part of the Church and the nation against her father. In the
country at large, outside the ranks of the conspiracy, men waited in
doubt, hesitation and sullen anger with the King, to see what the hour
would bring forth. For the moment there was no Royalist party at
all, not even among the clergy. Even after William had landed, the
Bishops, including several who afterwards became Jacobites, refused
the King's request to issue a pronouncement against rebellion. Non-
resistance had been the distinctive doctrine of the Anglican Church,
but in the month that mattered her clergy refused to proclaim it.

In the first days of November, William's Declaration, multiplied
by secret presses, was in the hands of the English, who stood watch-
ing the weathercocks for a "Protestant wind," whistling "Lillibul-
lero," or listening to the ballad-mongers' songs:

Good People, come buy
The fruit that I cry,
That now is in season tho' Winter be nigh;
'Twill do you all good,
And sweeten your blood,
I'm sure it will please you when once understood,
'Tis an Orange.

The agony of expectation was prolonged, while storms from the West delayed and battered William's fleet that was endeavouring to leave the coast of Holland. At length the wind shifted to the east and carried the new Armada westwards down-Channel towards the Devon coast, while it locked up the English fleet near the mouth of the Thames. Whether, if the wind had been favourable, any large section of the fleet would have obeyed Dartmouth's order to attack the Dutch, it is impossible to say. The matter was not put to the test. Thanks to the "Protestant" wind, William's landing at Torbay was carried out with no chance of molestation. The piety of the age saw William as the Deliverer favoured of heaven, the more so as he stepped ashore on November the Fifth, the day dedicated for many years past, by the services of the Church and by popular rites at nightfall, to thanksgiving for deliverance from the Popish designs of Guy Fawkes; the date was henceforth doubly marked with white in the recollection of English Protestants.

The army with which he landed was some 12,000 strong, much less than half the number of the regular forces in the pay of James. It was a cosmopolitan army, for the Dutch Republic recruited its troops from many different countries—Danes, Swedes, Germans, Swiss and French Huguenots, besides Hollanders. English and Scottish regiments were prominent in the van. It seemed a concourse of all the Protestant races of Europe come to help in the deliverance of England, rather than a Dutch invasion. The great banner that floated over the Prince's head as he marched, bore the time-honoured motto of the House of Orange, "I will maintain," with the timely addition of an accusative—"the Liberties of England and the Protestant religion."

As the troops struggled through the deep and muddy lanes of Devon, the country people greeted them with transports of delight, and the population of Exeter gave William a triumphal welcome into the capital of the West; but the magistrates of the City and the clergy of the Cathedral endeavoured not to commit themselves, and the Bishop fled to London, where he was rewarded by James by the Archbishopric of York. For a week no gentleman or person of note ventured to join the Prince. If he had landed without an army, a few troops of the royal horse could at this stage have chased him into the sea.

The reason of this initial delay in a rising that soon became so general was that William had not been expected in that part of England. It had been agreed that he should land in Yorkshire, where Danby stood prepared to raise the three Ridings as soon as the Prince set foot on the eastern coast. But since he had been forced to run before the wind to the South-West, a fortnight's delay took place before the Northern and Midland risings could be arranged in the absence of William. And in Devon the unexpected sight of the Prince and his troops could not at once relieve the fears engendered by the terrible vengeance that had followed Monmouth's rebellion in that region only three years before.

It was the common people who first welcomed the Prince. But after a short hesitation the leaders of the South-West, taking their cue from the popular enthusiasm, began to come in. The doctrine that the Revolution was "aristocratic" as distinct from popular is contradicted by all the facts. The mob, in town and country, was everywhere against James. But in Stuart England, specially since the Restoration of 1660, popular movements could only be effective if they were led by the upper class. It is impossible to say that one class favoured the Revolution more than another.

By the middle of November, from all parts of England Whig and Tory chiefs set out from their homes and rode with small groups of armed horsemen to join the Court and Camp at Exeter. The newcomers added little to the military strength of the rebellion, but enormously increased its political power. That was all William asked, for there was to be no fighting. The royal army was to be overpowered by the sense that the whole country was against the King.

Among those who joined William at Exeter was Sir Edward Seymour, the electoral King of the South-West, a Tory of Tories, a hater of Dissenters, but a Protestant and a Parliament man. His arrival and that of other high Royalists like the Earl of Abingdon and Clarendon's son Lord Cornbury, who led over the first small detachment of the King's army, were even more important than the arrival of Russells, Whartons and other Whig leaders which had been taken for granted. Whig and Tory formed one party at Exeter, and at

Seymour's suggestion signed an Association, binding themselves to pursue the objects of the Prince's Declaration, to stand by him and by each other, and, even if the Prince were killed, to avenge his death and secure the liberties and religion of the nation.

Thus was formed at Exeter, at the proposal of one of the strongest of High Churchmen and Tories, a united party that soon came to include the great majority of Englishmen, and was only dissolved when its object was achieved, and success led to divergence of opinion between Whig and Tory as to the precise nature of the Settlement to follow.

Meanwhile, Danby had reshaped his plans for the Northern insurrection, which had been thrown out by William's diversion to the South-West. On November 22 the conspirators seized York. The militia, gentry and populace of the Three Ridings were unanimous, and Danby led them with such ability and cunning that no resistance was put up by the King's servants and soldiers in the garrison towns. All Yorkshire passed without bloodshed into the hands of the Revolt. Lord Lumley overran Durham and entered Newcastle, where the mob threw James's statue into the Tyne. Howard, the Tory and Protestant Duke of Norfolk, seized Norwich and raised East Anglia for the Prince of Orange. Cavendish, the Whig Earl of Devonshire, seized Nottingham and raised the Midlands. The forces of the Midland rebellion were joined at Nottingham by the Princess Anne, James's second daughter, accompanied by her confidante, Sarah Churchill. The ladies came guarded by an improvised regiment of country gentlemen, under the command of the Church militant, in the person of Compton Bishop of London, formerly an officer of the Life Guards.

Even in these first whirling days, there were no scenes of blood. Even where the mob got loose without leaders to control it, houses of unpopular characters were sacked, and deer parks of Catholic gentry broken open, but no murder took place. The contrast to the atmosphere of the French Revolution is as striking in this as in other respects. And there was no fighting, for the King's partisans offered no resistance. In almost every region outside the range of the King's army the revolt had been successfully accomplished without bloodshed.

Yet the decision would lie in London and the Home Counties. The Capital and the South-East were passionately on the Prince's side, but they were for a short while longer restrained by the presence of the King's regular troops.

If, after the landing of William, James had been willing to come to an accommodation with his people, he would certainly have saved his throne at the price of abandoning his designs against the Church and the Constitution. The Tories, even those in arms against him, had at this stage no wish to dethrone him. He had only to summon a Parliament and submit to its decisions. The High Tory Lords and Bishops assembled in London besought him to issue writs for a general election and so put an end to all chance of civil war. But he answered that he would not call a Parliament until William and his army had left the island. To call a Parliament now would, he knew, be to surrender his schemes, though it would save his throne. He would not yield, he told his intimates, an atom, "no, not an atom." He would go to the front to take the chance of war. He left behind him in his capital, seething with disaffection, a council of five to represent him, of whom two were Roman Catholics, and one was the detested Chancellor Jeffreys. Thus he took the field, leaving the High Tory Lords and Bishops still unreconciled to his cause.

In this utterly recalcitrant mood he set off for the West, to put himself at the head of the advance guard of his troops at Salisbury, and lead them against the invader. William was still at Exeter, waiting there while the North, the Midlands and East Anglia rose. His great object was to avoid a battle and to give time for the movement of events to disintegrate the fighting force of the King.

On November 19, James reached Salisbury. During the week that he spent there with his troops, the issue of the campaign was decided, while the rival armies were still many miles apart. William, hearing that James was at Salisbury, began to move slowly forwards from Exeter, wisely sending his British troops in front. They skirmished with some of James's Irish at Wincanton, thus helping to make the invasion agreeable to the racial sensitiveness of the English. But no encounter of the least military importance took place. The war was won and lost in the camp at Salisbury, and in the mind and heart of James.

He found his troops in and around the Cathedral city, sullen, distracted, perhaps hostile. The news poured in that England north of Thames was rising against him. He became at last aware that many officers in the army, including, as he began to suspect, Churchill himself, were in secret league with William. He knew not whom to trust, for Churchill was one on whom he had heaped favours all his life. Some of his friends besought him to arrest the suspects, but he hesitated to precipitate the crisis. His health and nerves were shaken, and for three days he was confined to his room with a violent bleeding of the nose. When he recovered, he ordered a retreat to London; it amounted to an acknowledgment that William had won, and had the effect of dissolving what yet remained of the fabric of loyalty. Churchill, Grafton, Kirke and many others went straight over to William's camp. What was left of the army had lost all morale, and all desire to fight for a King who seemed equally incapable of treating or of fighting with his foes.

Thus England escaped a civil war. She owed this immense good fortune chiefly to two men, James and Churchill. At the crisis after William's landing the King had been obstinate as a statesman, yet spiritless and wavering as a soldier. He would not propitiate the moderates or summon Parliament, yet he had not dared to lead his troops to battle, fearing lest they should betray him. These fears were not ungrounded: the disintegration of the army was largely due to the conspiracy carried on for months before by Churchill in his position of second-in-command. In his own day, and ever since, many have called it unpardonable treachery in Churchill to remain in the King's service the better to betray him. Not only the Jacobites but the Whig historian Macaulay took this view. Yet the question remains open. Churchill had not, like Sunderland and others, kept his place by pretending to approve the King's policy; he had only pretended to be a loyal soldier. The essence of conspiracy is deceit. If, as Macaulay thought, conspiracy was justified by James's tyranny, what are the moral rules for conspiracy? They are not easy to define. Churchill's choice, right or wrong, saved England from civil war. It may have been the most equivocal but it was certainly not the least of the great services Marlborough did for England, that he remained in the royal service in order to betray the King who had betrayed his subjects; against the broken military oath of Churchill stood the broken Coronation Oath of the King. The rules for a man's conduct in time of revolution are not the rules of ordinary life. What they are it is difficult to say; and Englishmen have been blessed by not having to ask themselves the question since Christmas 1688.

When James returned to London, defeated without a battle, the issue was moved from the military to the political sphere. The King had been effectively disarmed. On December 2 Evelyn noted in his diary, "The Papists in office lay down their commissions and fly.

Universal consternation amongst them; it looks like a revolution."

All must now be settled by a freely elected Parliament. So much was clear, but all else was still in doubt. If James had himself summoned the Parliament, it would not have deposed him. If he had been prepared to abandon his designs and to become a constitutional monarch, neither the Whigs nor William could have turned him off the throne. For the Church and Tory party would never agree to downright deposition, in flat contradiction to their doctrine of the divine hereditary right of Kings. James could have been deposed only by civil war, which the Englishmen of that generation, taught by their fathers' experience, were determined to avoid. But he dethroned himself by flying to France; and he dethroned his heirs after him by sending the baby Prince of Wales to be brought up a Roman Catholic at the French Court. He left the Tories no choice but to adopt the Whig policy of settling the Crown on William and Mary; and the Revolution thus reached its consummation in a dynastic change.

The flight of James was a personal choice not imposed on him by circumstances. It was bitterly regretted by all his friends, Catholic and Protestant, except the small Jesuit and Francophil group who had led him to destruction. The flight greatly diminished the chance of civil war by depriving the Tories of a standpoint on which to resist the Whig desire for a change of King; and it drove the great majority of those who had lately been Royalists on to the Whig platform. It dictated the form that the Revolution Settlement had necessarily to take.

Having sent his wife and infant son before him to the protection of Louis of France, James prepared to follow them himself. To cover his real purpose, he sent Halifax and other noblemen to William's camp at Hungerford, commissioned to treat with the Prince for the election and summons of a Free Parliament. While this sham negotiation was going on at Hungerford, James stole out from Whitehall at three in the morning of December 11, and drove along the south bank of the river to the Isle of Sheppey in Kent, where a small ship was waiting, ready to carry him to France. He left behind him no powers of Regency for the government of the country. He destroyed the writs for a new Parliament, he sunk the Great Seal in the Thames, and left orders for the disbandment of the army. His object was to leave England in a state of anarchy, which would facilitate his victorious return at the head of a French army, or at the summons of a repentant people.

On December 12, 1688, the country awoke to find itself without a government. On the following night London was in the hands of raging mobs, who sacked and burnt the mansions and chapels of the Roman Catholics. But no lives were taken, and the further spread of anarchy was stopped by prompt action. The City fathers and those Lords and magnates who happened to be in London, including Archbishop Sancroft and others who afterwards became Jacobites and Non-jurors, constituted themselves an improvised committee of public safety, took steps for restoring order in the Capital and invited William to hasten to their aid. Halifax, and all the moderates who had been trying to negotiate a compromise, threw in their lot with the Prince of Orange once for all. James had by his flight forced the whole country to rally to his rival's standard as the only way to preserve law and property from mob rule. As Lady Dartmouth wrote from London: "Lord Chandseler (Jeffreys) is prisener in the Tower, and the rable ready to pull him to peces. Indeed this town as bin mighty unquiat since the King's departure, by pulling the chapells down and houses of papists and imbassadors, so that every body is in great frights and wish for the Prince of Oringe coming to quiat things."

Again James had cleared the way for his rival. But here the course of events, gliding towards an unexpectedly peaceful and rapid solution, encountered an equally unexpected obstacle arising from the merest accident. While James was weatherbound off the Isle of Sheppey, the vessel in which he had embarked was boarded by one of the mobs who had everywhere risen as the news of the King's flight spread. The fishermen searched the ship, mistook the King for a Jesuit escaping to France, pulled him about roughly, and carried him ashore as their captive.

His identity became known and the news that the King was a prisoner in rude hands soon reached the Capital, causing a natural revulsion of pity, and a hope in many breasts that he might yet come back and submit to reign according to law.

William had not yet reached London: if he had been there, he would no doubt have sent down orders into Kent that James should be released and that the ship should have free passage to carry him away. But London was still in the hands of the self-constituted Committee of Lords, who did not know what to do in a situation so strange, and many of whom wished James to return and become a Constitutional King. James's best friends, Lords Aylesbury and Feversham, were sent to conduct him back to his capital. Aylesbury arrived first and found him among his captors "sitting in a great chair, his hat on, and his beard being much grown, and resembled the picture of his royal father at the pretended High Court of Justice. He took me to a window with an air of displeasure and said, 'You were all Kings when I left London.'" This was too much even for the faithful Aylesbury, who replied, "Give me leave to tell your Majesty that [on] your going away without leaving a Commission of Regency, but for our care and vigilance the city of London might have been in ashes."

A troop of Life Guards accompanied James back to Whitehall with royal honours. As he passed through the City, the mob, who had lately been sacking the houses of his co-religionists, received the returning Monarch with cheers, prompted partly by pity for fallen greatness and the rough usage he had met with from the Kentish fishermen, and partly by a hope that the King was returning to rule thenceforward according to the laws of the land.

Accident had given James a last chance to come to terms with his subjects; but he had no such thought in his heart. He was still set on reaching France, and his second flight was speeded by the policy of William, who not only put every convenience in his way to make a second departure easy and secure, but took harsher steps undoubtedly meant to frighten away the King. Though regicide was the crime most abhorrent to that generation of Englishmen, James, as he told Aylesbury, was afraid of the fate of Charles I if he remained in England. William had no wish to remove these idle fears, though violence to the King's person was the last thing of which he dreamt. He changed his policy of magnanimity for one of sternness. Up till the return of James to London, William, though military victor, had consented to treat his defeated rival as a political equal, and in the negotiations at Hungerford had not even demanded to occupy London during the general election. But after the King's first flight, after the Tory Lords in London had invited the Prince of Orange to enter the Capital, he was not going to be deterred by the accident of his rival's enforced return. The position was not to be put back where it had been the week before.

William therefore sent his blue Dutch Guards to occupy the posts at Whitehall Palace, in place of James's own English Guards, thereby assuming control over the King's movements. He then ordered his rival to quit London before he himself made entry. It was arranged that James should reside at Rochester, it being well understood that a seaside place was chosen in order that the flight to France should be resumed and not again be interrupted. He was carried down the river guarded by the Dutch bluecoats as far as Rochester, and there set at liberty in a house upon the shore of the Medway. At midnight of December 22, he stole away once more, never again to set foot in the island.

Thus the accidental interruption of the King's first flight did not prevent his final departure or alter the nature of the Revolution Settlement. But it caused the first reaction of sentiment in favour of James whence the Jacobite party drew its being. Henceforth it might be argued that he had been forced to fly, though in fact his flight had been his fixed and voluntary purpose. And the sight of the blue Dutch Guards replacing the red-coats round the King's Palace and conducting a King of England down the Thames, had not been pleasant. The fact was that during the winter of the Revolution the English Army, distracted by rival loyalties, could be trusted neither by William nor by James. Though James could not venture to lead it to battle, it was at least more Jacobite than the rest of the nation. When the Prince of Orange made his triumphal entry into London on December 18, 1688, he was adored by the English people and disliked by the English Army. Ten years later the exact opposite was the case. For though William was very much greater as a statesman than as a general, yet his cold ungracious manner soon alienated the love of his English subjects, while his gallant comradeship in the field won the hearts of his soldiers in Ireland and Flanders.

James having been finally disposed of by his second flight, the country had to supply itself with a government. There was no legal authority in England, and civil war would grow out of anarchy unless a prompt settlement were made; in Scotland civil war was practically certain in any case; Ireland, loyal to James, was preparing to exterminate the last resistance of the English colonists in the Ulster; and Louis of France, with his greet fleets and armies, had espoused the cause of the exiled King. At this terrible crisis, the instinct of the English for improvised political action was seen at its best. Before Christmas, those members of the House of Lords and of the Commons Houses of Charles II's reign, who could be assembled at once in London, met to consult for the safety of the Kingdom, and requested the Prince of Orange to take over the administration of

England, and to summon a Convention Parliament. A similar request was made by the notables of Scotland on behalf of the sister Kingdom. William took up the assigned task; quelled anarchy in England; protected the Roman Catholics against further violence; borrowed money from the City for the immediate needs of the State; confirmed the authority of magistrates and law courts, lapsed by the disappearance of the King; rallied under his own command the English and Scottish regiments of the disbanded royal army; sent out of the island the Irish troops, whose presence was causing widespread panic; and, last but not least, issued letters for the immediate election and meeting next month of the Convention Parliament, which was to dispose of the throne and settle the future of England.

There was no legal validity in the power of a Prince thus irregularly entrusted with functions that belonged to the Crown, but as there was no longer any legal authority in the land after the King's flight, the Prince's orders were universally obeyed. The question who should fill the throne was left over to the meeting of the Convention Parliament, which the Prince had now summoned. But the fact that he was conducting the provisional government with success during Christmas 1688, accustomed men to the idea that he and his wife should be made King and Queen, when the Parliament that he had summoned should meet in the following month.

If James had remained in England and submitted to be King under the tutelage of Parliament, it is probable that the change made by the Revolution in the forms of our Constitution would have been greater than it actually was. James would not have been trusted again, without defined limitations to his power. But since William was put on the throne, it was not thought necessary to tie his hands by quasi-republican restrictions on his free action. William, for instance, continued, like all previous Kings, to choose his own Ministers, nominate the Judges and magistrates, and the officers of the Army and Navy. This freedom of action left to the new King did indeed bring him into frequent conflicts with the House of Commons in the latter part of his reign. And the friction between Crown and Commons gradually led to important changes not indeed in the law but in the custom of the Constitution. In the reign of William, Anne and George I the Constitution began to move, under the impulse given by the Revolution, in the direction of the modern Cabinet system, which enables the leaders of Parliament to choose and conduct the royal policy and nominate the royal servants. But this change was neither desired nor foreseen by anyone in 1689. And it has been a change not in law but in custom. In the eye of the law the King to this day retains executive powers much like those of the Tudor monarchs, though in fact the exercise of these powers has long since been delegated to Cabinet Ministers representing the majority in the House of Commons.

But if James had chosen to remain as King after the Revolution, it is highly probable that the royal authority in these matters would have been circumscribed by restrictive laws. No one would have trusted him again in his old position. He would certainly have been supplied with Ministers not of his own choice, and the Crown patronage in Church and State would have been taken out of his hands. We should have had something much more like a written Constitution. We were saved by James's flight to France from the necessity of making any such formal change in the law of the Constitution, which would have proved in practice a very clumsy and possibly a disastrous experiment.

Thus the slight change that was effected in the order of succession at the expense of James and his son, although it was the most revolutionary aspect of the Revolution, was in fact the necessary condition of its otherwise conservative character.

The Revolution Settlement of Church and State, which we have now to examine, lasted with very little statutory change down to the era of Reform in the nineteenth century, and its main principles still underlie the democratic and bureaucratic institutions that have since been reared on its foundation. This Settlement arose out of the situation created by the flight of James, but the form that it took was the deliberate choice and act of the Convention Parliament.

What precisely was the "Convention Parliament"? It had been summoned by letters issued at Christmas by the Prince of Orange at the request of the unofficial assembly of Peers and former members of the Commons. The elections for it took place during the Interregnum, on the authority of these letters of the Prince; they were not proper writs such as only a King could issue, for there was no King. The first business of the Convention would be to provide a King. Therefore the two Houses that met in January were not a Parliament in the strict letter of the law. They were merely a "Convention" like that which had summoned home Charles II in 1660. This fact gave to the Jacobites their legal standpoint whence to impugn the title of William and Mary as King and Queen, since their title derived from the act of this irregular "Convention". The title of Charles II had not, in the eye of the law, derived from the Convention of 1660, but from his own hereditary right.

Here, then, lay the revolutionary and extra-legal basis of all that was done in 1689. It was impossible to avoid a flaw in the legal title of a Parliament summoned and chosen during an Interregnum, for the English Constitution cannot function legally without a King.

None the less, the Revolution Settlement was first and foremost the establishment of the rule of law. It was the triumph of the Common Law and lawyers over the King, who had tried to put Prerogative above the law. Henceforth the law could only be altered by Statutes passed in Parliament by the action of both Houses with the consent of the King. And the interpretation of the law was henceforth left to law courts freed by the Revolution from all governmental interference, on the new principle of the irremovability of Judges. Apart from the dynastic change, which coloured everything in the new era, there were only two new principles of any importance introduced in 1689. One was that the Crown could not remove Judges; the other was that Protestant Dissenters were to enjoy toleration for their religious worship. Almost everything else was, nominally at least, only restoration, to repair the breaches in the constitutional fabric made by the illegalities of James II. But in fact the struggle between King and Parliament had been for ever decided.

The liberal-conservative character of the Revolution Settlement must be sought in the character of the House of Commons elected in January 1689. How and in what spirit was that House chosen? What, if any, were the instructions given to its members by their constituents?

The elections to the Convention Parliament took place under abnormal conditions. There was no King and no regular government. The country was in the greatest danger of internal convulsion and foreign conquest, and the national crisis loomed larger in men's minds than the usual Whig and Tory nonsense. An anxious, sober patriotism was the spirit of the hour. Moreover, the Whigs and Tories had for some time past been acting together as one party against James and had not yet had time to fly asunder and resume their old quarrels.

This state of things at the New Year affected the character of the General Election. In the first place, since there was no King, no royal influence was exerted on behalf of candidates even in the regular "government boroughs" like the Cinque Ports. And in ordinary constituencies, those many electors and borough patrons who usually gave their votes and influence in hope of places, pensions or royal favour, were on this occasion left to their own devices; for no one knew who was to be King, still less who were to be his Ministers. Never was a general election so free from government influence as that which returned the Commons House of 1689.

Secondly, the elections were conducted with less than usual of the animosity of faction. Whigs were returned and Tories, but so far as we know without bitter conflict; the bitterest conflicts between candidates of which we have evidence were due to the local rivalry of families and persons. In every Parliament of the next twenty years there were members who were neither Whigs nor Tories; and this unattached element was specially large in the Convention, elected to meet a national emergency that transcended party.

Moreover, those members who were definitely Whig or Tory had not pledged themselves at the elections to any precise programme, as for instance many of the members chosen at the election of 1681 had been pledged and instructed to support the Exclusion Bill. In 1689 no such instructions and pledges appear to have been exchanged between the candidates and the electors. The members chosen were stout Protestants, sent up to save the religion and constitution of the country in such way as should seem best to them in London, when they had taken stock of a situation of unparalleled difficulty. The electors had the prudence to leave the solution to the unfettered wisdom of Parliament. This explains why the Convention was guided more by common sense than by party prejudice, why, for instance, it settled the dynastic question mainly on Whig lines, and the ecclesiastical settlement mainly on Tory lines, because such proved the best and safest way to give peace to the land.

Indeed, the most remarkable feature of the elections was the silence observed about the greatest question of the hour. Everyone knew that the first duty of the Convention would be to decide who was to be King or Queen. Everyone also knew that on this matter grave differences of opinion were latent and would soon emerge. The London presses, released by the Interregnum from all censorship, were pouring forth pamphlets on every side of the question. But candidates and electors throughout the country appear to have felt that the filling of the throne was a matter too deep and dangerous to be propounded on the hustings. No pledges were demanded, and so far as we know no election speeches or promises were made on this all-important issue. Members went up to the great inquest of the nation free to examine and solve the problem there. The decision to make William and Mary joint King and Queen was not taken at the polls; the issue was raised and was decided in the Convention Parliament by men who had made no promises to their constituents, except to save the country and re-establish the Constitution as best they could.[1]

The members of the Convention met with friendly dispositions towards one another. They had been acting together against James up to the moment of his flight; since then both parties had united to request William to assume the administration; the general election had not borne the character of a fierce party contest. As soon as the Lords and Commons began to take stock of the problems that they met to solve, the divisions of Whig and Tory naturally reappeared; but the wonder is not that there were differences, but that the differences were settled by agreement so promptly and with so much goodwill and readiness to compromise.

The tone of the Convention of 1689 was very different from that of the Cavalier Parliament that had passed the Clarendon Code against the Puritans, or of the Whig Parliaments that had followed the wild leading of Shaftesbury. During the first six months of its existence, the Convention Parliament showed much more patriotism than party spirit. Both sides made concessions, under the pressure of national danger, and at the urgency of the large section in both Houses who were neither Tory nor Whig. It was in those six months that the Revolution Settlement took the shape that proved permanent, not as a triumph of one party over the other, but as an agreed compromise between Whig and Tory, Church and Dissent.

The first business of the Convention was to decide who should fill the throne, and on that issue the new Whig and the new Tory parties came into existence. Yet the differences of parties on the dynastic question arose from a difference of theory rather than of practice. Both sides desired William to stay in England as head of the administration. The question in dispute was by what right and with what title he should bear rule.

The Tory politicians and the Anglican clergy in Charles II's reign had pledged themselves repeatedly to the theory of divine hereditary right of Kings and non-resistance of subjects. They had since been compelled to resist James II, in spite of all their theories, because they were men. But also because they were men, they could not all

[1] For the elections to the Convention Parliament, see the article by J. H. Plumb in the *Cambridge Historical Journal*, 1937.

of them at once abandon the whole set of associated ideas in which they had been brought up. They could not, as quickly as the Vicar of Bray, treat "passive obedience as a jest" and make "a joke of non-resistance." They set themselves therefore to explain away the Revolution while reaping its fruits in practice. They desired to make such a settlement of the Crown as would not be in too obvious contradiction of the doctrines which they had all so recently proclaimed, and which many of them still loved and reverenced. They asserted, to begin with, that James had never been driven away, but that he had voluntarily deserted his functions. They had risen against him in arms, meaning only to bring him to reason, and he had, instead of submitting, fled oversea to the national enemy. The blessed word "abdicate" would save his subjects from the sin of having deposed him. James had "abdicated" the government. And further, the Tories hoped that a little ingenuity could surely be used to avoid a breach in the divinely appointed order of hereditary succession.

Such was the nature of Tory anxieties when the Convention met in January 1689.

The Whigs, on the other hand, thought that a slight change in the order of succession would be a good thing in itself, because it would kill the Stuart theory of divine hereditary right. It would make the title to the Crown a Parliamentary title, to the same extent as in Plantagenet and Tudor days, when Parliament had several times disposed of the Crown, not always to the nearest of kin. The Whigs believed that such another Parliamentary gift of the Crown would establish their own theory of the contract between King and People, involving the forfeiture of the Crown in case of breach of that contract. Only so, thought the Whigs, could the limited nature of the monarchy be secured for all time. No doubt the Tories of 1689, like the Cavaliers of 1640 and 1660, wished the powers of the Crown to be limited in practice. But was such a Constitutional practice consonant with a theory suited only to despotism? For if the King continued, in the eyes of half his subjects, to hold a quasi-divine office by inheritance, how was a mere earthly Parliament to limit his supernatural rights whenever he chose to insist on them? A divine monarchy must always override a mere human Parliament. Since monarchy and Parliament could not both be divine in men's eyes, let them both, said the Whigs, be human, and here is our great opportunity to make them so.

On this deeply important principle the two parties, otherwise friendly for the moment, found themselves divided in the debates and divisions of February 1689. The Whigs had several decisive advantages. They were in high spirits over the Regifuge, and were united on a single proposal to give their principles effect. They wanted to declare the throne vacant and to put William and Mary together into the vacancy, by an Act of Parliament. The Tories, on the other hand, were divided and uneasy, occupying a position as rebels from which they would fain retreat, if only they could retire with the fruits of rebellion in their hands.

The flight of the King, sending before him the infant heir to be brought up as a Roman Catholic under the influences of the French Court, made all Tory solutions of the crisis impracticable. The Tories were divided between three proposals, each intended to save the moribund principle of divine right. These proposals were:

(1) To recall James on conditions—but James would accept no conditions, so only the Jacobites ultimately supported this proposal.

(2) To make William Regent, nominally in James's name, but really against James's authority.

(3) To declare Mary Queen in her own right, with her husband as Prince Consort or King Consort.

The Regency of William in King James's name had been proposed as a possible compromise at the time of the Exclusion Controversy of Charles II's reign. But it must be noted that at that time James had no children except his Protestant daughters, Mary and Anne; whereas in 1689 James's heir was an infant son, in the hands of the French Jesuits and the French King. Unless, therefore, the Tories were going to rest their whole case on the alleged supposititious character of the new baby, they would have been bound, under the Regency plan, to acknowledge the Old and Young Pretender in succession as titular Kings of England. Generation after generation, throughout the eighteenth century, successive Regents of England would have had to wage war on the acknowledged King of England supported by the power of France. England, in fact, would have become a Republic, if she did not submit to a Jacobite restoration. It is then no wonder that the Regency plan, put forward by Archbishop Sancroft and the High Church Bishops to save their consciences, was not favourably looked on by Tory statesmen like Danby, and was voted down even in the House of Lords, where the Tories had a predominance.

It would be necessary, in order to place William and Mary on the throne by a Parliamentary Act, to declare the throne vacant. But the Tory Lords, led by Danby, resisted the vacancy of the throne as long as they could do so without endangering the public safety. For they saw that, if they once admitted that the throne could at any time be vacant, they destroyed the conception of divine hereditary right; if the regal power came from God it must always be vested in some person without the help of Parliament or Convention. The moment one person ceased to be King, another was in his place by divine right. Nature abhors a vacuum, and divine right abhors a vacancy. "Le roi est mort, vive le roi." Therefore Danby's view was that James had "abdicated" the government by his flight, and that his daughter Mary should be held to have thereby and at that moment succeeded in her own hereditary right; and so, said Danby, there was no "vacancy" of the throne. This view ignored Mary's baby brother James. Since the baby was in France, he could not be brought up as a Protestant. Let him then be passed over in silence, in the hope that he was supposititious, since none but Papists saw him born. Such was Danby's device to save the Divine Hereditary Right of Kings, even at the moment of the armed Revolution of which he had been the chief English leader. Danby saw that the plan of Regency was impossible, but he put forward Mary as the sole heir by right divine. But Danby's plan would not save divine right, except by the official adoption of the warming-pan legend.

The Whigs defeated Danby, for on this issue they obtained a majority in the Commons; non-party members realized that the Tory proposal was impracticable. And the Lords, after some days of resistance, submitted to the will of the Commons rather than leave the country to drift kingless into anarchy. Danby indeed discovered that his own plan was impossible, because neither William nor Mary would consent to play the parts allotted them under the scheme. Mary refused to be Queen unless her husband was King. And William for his part would not accept the position of Prince or King Consort under his wife. He would not, he said, be her gentleman usher. Moreover, Englishmen in general felt that the distracted British Islands could only be saved from James and Louis by strong administration, and that William alone was capable, by his talents, experience and European position, of providing that strong administration in home and foreign affairs. Indeed, the Tories recognized that no less than the Whigs. But to save their own theories they wished him to administer the country in the name of his wife as the sole sovereign. William thought that in so equivocal a position he would not have authority enough to deal with the crisis—and, in fact, he only just managed to weather it with the full authority of King. Therefore, the practical needs of the nation at that hour dictated the acceptance of the Whig plan with all the advantages or disadvantages of its theoretic implications.

One important concession was made to the Tory view. James was declared to have "abdicated" the government by his voluntary flight. He was not declared to have been "deposed," nor to have "forfaulted," that is "forfeited," the Crown as the Scottish Convention at Edinburgh pronounced, in its more thorough-going Whig manner.

On these terms the Tories in both Houses abandoned the struggle and agreed to the Whig proposal to declare the throne vacant. The word "vacant" destroyed divine hereditary right in the realm of theory, and in practice made it possible to crown William on equal terms with his wife. They were made joint sovereigns, reigning side by side. Their heads appeared together on the coinage. That being settled, the administration was by general consent vested in William during his life. For the Tories had all along desired his administration, even while on theoretical grounds they had deprecated his Kingship.

The Commons' formula, to which the Lords finally agreed, ran as follows:

That King James the Second, having endeavoured to subvert the Constitution of the Kingdom, by breaking the *Original Contract* between King and people [a Whig remark], and by the advice of Jesuits and other wicked persons having violated the fundamental laws and withdrawn himself out of the Kingdom, hath *abdicated* the government [a concession to the Tories] and that *the throne is thereby vacant* [a Whig conclusion].

The acceptance by Whigs and Tories of this formula and their acknowledgment of William and Mary as joint King and Queen by Act of Parliament saved the country from anarchy and civil war, and frustrated the plans of Louis of France by putting back a united England upon the map of Europe.

Both parties and both Houses agreed without division in the further conclusion—

That it hath been found by experience to be inconsistent with this Protestant Kingdom to be governed by a Popish Prince.

That principle was drafted into a law, which is to this day the law of the land. No Roman Catholic or person married to a Roman Catholic can wear the crown.

The Tories, as distinct from the Jacobites, loyally served William as King. Danby, to whom the disputes in the Convention had been an affair of politics, not of religion, accepted William without reserve, and became his loyal subject and servant. He looked with contempt on the scruples of the Non-jurors, who refused to swear allegiance to the new sovereigns. But the other chief Tory leader, Nottingham, was a religious man first and foremost, and he, like other Anglicans, had been brought up to think divine hereditary right a part of religion. He therefore accepted William as King *de facto* and by law, but not *de jure*, by right—a distinction recognized and encouraged by an old English law of Henry VII's reign. The new oaths of allegiance were drawn up to meet the scruples of the *de facto* Tories; by the oath as it was framed in 1689 they were not asked to call William "rightful" King, but only to accept him as King in fact. William, in nominating Nottingham on these terms as one of his chief Ministers, said emphatically that he was "an honest man." So he was. He never intrigued with the exiled court at St. Germains, but remained more scrupulously faithful to William, his King *de facto,* than some of his more easy-going Whig and Tory colleagues to William their King *de jure.*

But the theoretical objection to what had taken place in the winter 1688-9 continued intermittently to disturb the minds of Tories. Their conscience, and particularly the conscience of the clergy, was kept uneasy by the taunts of those of their old friends who had become Jacobites and Non-jurors. The "Non-jurors" were 400 beneficed clergy, including five out of the Seven Bishops who had been prosecuted by James, who now refused to take the oaths to William and Mary and had therefore to relinquish their livings and Sees. "Politically," says Mr. Keith Feiling, "the 'Non-jurors' influence was portentous, and constantly dragged their old party back to the causes lost."

This uneasiness of the Tory, and particularly of the clerical, conscience, and the uncertain and wavering character of Tory sympathies in relation to the exiled James and his son and grandson, constitute a fact of great historical importance. It governs the story of the fortunes of parties down to the end of the reign of George II. It originated in the proceedings of the winter of 1688-9. The

Revolution had made the Tories a Parliamentary and Constitutional party for all time to come; but it also made them, for two generations to come, a party with a poor logical position and an uneasy mind, often divided into opposite camps at a crisis. These circumstances diminished the power of the Tory body, which was normally the strongest in the State, containing as it did the great majority of the squires and almost all the parish clergy. At the crisis at Anne's death in 1714 the dynastic question paralysed and divided the Tories and gave to their rivals forty years of power under George I and II. But during the reigns of William and Anne power was fairly equally divided between Tories and Whigs.

William and Mary were not made King and Queen without conditions. The instrument by which the Convention raised them to the throne was the famous Declaration of Right. It made a long recital of the various illegal acts of James, more especially his claim to suspend the laws by Prerogative; it declared all these actions to have been illegal, and it required the acceptance of these limitations of the royal power by the new sovereigns as a condition of their elevation to the throne.

The solemn interview between the Prince and Princess of Orange, and the Houses of Parliament with Halifax as their spokesman, was held at Whitehall on February 13, 1689. The scene was the Banqueting House, from a window of which Charles I had stepped out on to the scaffold. In that great hall William and Mary accepted from the Houses of Lords and Commons the Crown and the Declaration of Right together. At this happier ceremony there were no "armèd bands" or "forcèd power." An agreed contract was freely made between Crown and people which prevented for all time to come a repetition of the tragedies of the Stuart Kings. The pendulum-swing of alternate violence of rebels and royalists was slowed down to the gentler oscillation of rival Parliamentary parties. And what the Crown lost in power it gained in security. The Republican movement was buried, not to revive in England in any formidable manner either at the time of the French Revolution, or with the coming of social democracy in the nineteenth and twentieth centuries. England had acquired the outline of a Constitution in which she could work out her remoter destinies.

The Declaration of Right was, in form at least, purely conservative. It introduced no new principle of law, not even Toleration for

Dissenters or irremovability of Judges, though there was entire agreement on the immediate necessity of those two reforms. For the Convention had wisely decided that alterations in the existing laws would require time for debate, and not another day could be spared before the throne was filled, without great risk to the public safety. Therefore the Declaration of Right had been framed as a mere recital of those existing rights of Parliament and of the subject, which James had outraged, and which William must promise to observe. All further changes, however pressing their need, must wait till Parliament should have time to discuss and pass them, and till there was a King to give them statutory force by royal assent to new laws.

The first Act to which William and Mary consented after coming to the throne was an Act converting the Convention into a Parliament, for since there was now a King, there could be a Parliament. And the Declaration of Right was subsequently reenacted as a Parliamentary Statute.

The Convention, having thus filled the throne and converted itself, in so far as it was possible to do so, into a legal Parliament, proceeded to legislate. Only less important than the dynastic question was the religious question. Until the relation of Church and Dissent, of Anglican and Puritan, had been adjusted in a way tolerable to both parties, the Revolution Settlement was incomplete, and the country would still be liable to violent disturbance in the future. The Toleration Act of May 1689, which granted the right of free public worship to Protestant Dissenters, settled the question by a lasting compromise, and moderated the undying strife of Church and Dissent by removing from it the element of direct religious persecution.

The sufferings of the Protestant Dissenters ever since the Restoration had, with occasional intervals, been very severe. Under the "Clarendon Code" of persecuting laws, their ministers, like John Bunyan, had been kept in gaol for years; their religious services, held in secret, had often been discovered and broken up, and the congregations swept off to prison; their schools were closed and their schoolmasters forbidden to teach; and ruinous fines were often inflicted for nonconformity. It was the least of their grievances that they were excluded from the Universities, the public services, and the municipal government of the towns in which they were often the leading citizens. This whole code of religious persecution and civil disability had been swept away by James's illegal Declaration of Indulgence in 1687. Some of the Puritans had in return supported him; but more had hesitated to betray the Constitution, and were won over to the national cause by the solemn promise of the Tory leaders and High Church Bishops that they would support a Bill to relieve them from persecution directly a free Parliament should meet.

On this understanding the main body of the Dissenters had opposed James in 1688, and now the time had come for the Tories and Churchmen to fulfil their promise made in the hour of need. Nottingham, the recognized representative of the Church in Parliament, himself laid the Toleration Bill of May 1689 on the table of the House of Lords. It was largely of his drafting and was an agreed measure. The principle of toleration for Protestant Dissenters had long been advocated by the Whigs and opposed by the Tories. Now, in consequence of the abnormal events of James II's reign, a Tory chief introduced the Bill and both parties accepted it without demur.

Religious persecution of Protestant Dissenters was brought to an end, but not their civil disabilities. The Church retained its monopoly of the Universities, of the Crown Service and of Municipal Offices to the same extent as before. The Prayer Book was not altered to admit even the more orthodox Dissenters into the fold of the Established Church. In short, the Ecclesiastical Settlement of 1689 was a compromise inclining to the Church and Tory side of things, whereas the Dynastic Settlement had inclined to the Whig side.

It was this element of prudent compromise, preferring fact to theory and recognizing and respecting the strength of existing parties in Church and State, that saved the Revolution Settlement from reversal and saved England from civil war in the years to come. In Scotland, where the Revolution Settlement was an out-and-out triumph of Whig and Presbyterian over Tory and Episcopalian, the Tories all became Jacobites and civil war was endemic for the next sixty years. In Ireland, Whigs and Tories combined to oppress the native population more cruelly than ever before.

The Toleration Act has proved one of the most lastingly successful measures ever passed by Parliament. So far as England is concerned, it closed for ever the long chronicle of religious persecution and religious war. This was no small achievement, if we consider what was happening in that same era in France, and in Ireland, and what has since happened in those two countries.

The success of the Toleration Act was in part due to its limitations. It had been drawn up with great practical skill and prudence, so as to win the consent of all parties, to relieve the timid and to placate the prejudiced. Its limitations, its illogicality, its want of theoretical principle which made it acceptable in that bygone age, amuse or irritate the modern student, if he judges its provisions by the standards of our own day.

No general principle of Toleration is announced. Indeed, the suspected word "Toleration" is nowhere to be found in the measure which subsequent generations have agreed to call "the Toleration Act," but which the Members of Parliament who debated it called "the Bill of Indulgence." Its full title was "An Act for exempting their Majesties' Protestant Subjects, differing from the Church of England, from the Penalties of certain Laws." The Preamble states its limited and purely practical object:

Forasmuch as some ease to scrupulous consciences in the exercise of religion may be an effectual means to unite their Majesties' protestant subjects in interest and affection . . .

The Clarendon Code of persecuting laws is not repealed, but certain classes of people on certain conditions are allowed to claim exemption from the most oppressive of those laws. All who will take the Oaths of Allegiance and Supremacy and the Oath against Transubstantiation need not attend Church and may attend public worship in their own Conventicles.

So much for the laity: as to the Nonconformist clergy, they can obtain relief from the laws oppressing them, provided they sign thirty-four of the thirty-nine Articles of Religion in the Prayer Book, and part of two other Articles. This sounds oppressive, but in fact the doctrinal Articles they were required to sign were those with which the principal Dissenting Sects were in agreement. Other clauses made special provision for the benefit of the Baptists and for the benefit of the Quakers. Two religious bodies obtained no relief under the Toleration Act—the Roman Catholics, who were certain to be hostile to the new regime, and the Unitarians, who were regarded as heretics outside the pale.

To the modern mind this all seems silly and ungracious. Yet a more liberal and thorough-going Bill would either not have passed or would soon have been repealed. It was no easy task to persuade Tories to accept Toleration for Protestant Dissenters at all. And it would have been impossible to induce either Tories or Whigs, immediately after their experience with James II, to grant legal relief to Roman Catholics. Neither the Church nor the general religious conscience of the nation accepted religious tolerance as a principle of universal application. But in fact, by this careful picking of steps in a slippery path, England advanced further towards Toleration in practice than any other European country except Holland.

John Locke, the great political philosopher of the age, had written a *Letter concerning Toleration*. It appeared in English for the first time some months after the Toleration Act had been passed. That famous letter made admirably clear to the general intelligence the argument for universal religious Toleration, as a duty obligatory on every Christian State, and a personal right that could not be denied to any law-abiding citizen. The same large view was held by William Penn and the Quakers, but by very few other religious people. Neither Anglican nor Puritan when in power had tolerated the other. As a general rule, only the sceptical were heartily for Toleration; but the numbers of the partially sceptical, the "latitudinarians," were in that age upon the increase.

Locke obtained a dominating influence over men's minds in the generation that followed, a generation which found by experience that religious toleration gave peace to the land. The wide acceptance of his philosophy in the latitudinarian era now setting in prevented the repeal of the Toleration Act and gradually enlarged its scope and application. Yet it is well worth observing that, though Locke was in advance of average opinion in 1689, even he declared in his Letter that Atheists should not be tolerated, because they must necessarily deny the principles of virtue on which society rests; and that Roman Catholics, though they might be tolerated in practice, have no absolute claim to Toleration in so far as they hold the doctrine of keeping no faith with heretics or acknowledge the supremacy of another ruler.

In 1689 the Toleration Act was accepted, not on general or theoretic grounds, but as a political compromise rendered necessary by certain practical considerations, which had their full weight in a generation less cocksure on rival points of religious doctrine than the men who had drawn sword in 1642. Ever since the Restoration, statesmen and publicists had been lamenting the injury done to trade, especially in London, by the persecution of Puritan manufacturers and merchants; public opinion had grown to dislike the whole business of persecuting Protestants; Churchmen were bound to fulfil the promise of statutory relief that they had made to Dissenters to outbid James's illegal Declaration of Indulgence; and now that the Revolution had actually taken place, it was a matter of urgency to unite all their Majesties' Protestant subjects in defence of the new regime against its numerous enemies at home and abroad. The Act of Toleration had therefore been drawn up by Nottingham to give relief to Protestant Dissenters, with as little change as possible in theory or in law. It was a Bill embodying Whig principles in a modified form, introduced by a Tory statesman, and accepted by both parties. Therefore the Tories never tried to repeal it. But the High Churchmen and hotter Tories never liked it. They were perpetually trying to limit its action by measures like the Occasional Conformity Bill of Anne's reign, or to turn its flank by the short-lived Schism Act of 1714.

But the High Tory dislike of Toleration proved only a rear-guard action. The old religious feuds, though still the driving force in our party politics, became less fierce than before, when the element of religious persecution had been removed. The spirit of the new age ushered in by the Revolution, the Latitudinarianism of the eighteenth century with Locke and Newton for its philosophers, confirmed and enlarged those religious liberties which had been gained in 1689 as the accidental outcome of a strange political crisis. Indeed, the practice of the new age extended the principle of Toleration of religious rites to Roman Catholics and Unitarians, although they had been deliberately excluded from the benefits of the Toleration Act.

The Roman Catholic body in England after the reign of James II was so feeble and so unpopular that it might safely have been persecuted. But William disliked persecution, and he required the alliance of the Emperor and the King of Spain, and the support of the Pope in the struggle against France. He therefore made himself the protector of the Roman Catholics in England. He admitted none of them to office contrary to the law; but he discouraged informers and prosecutions, so that in fact Mass was said in private houses with more and more freedom. In ordinary years Parliament made no demand that the laws against the Roman Catholic worship should be enforced. From time to time, when a Jacobite plot was detected, or a French invasion was expected, the laws were set in operation to hunt out and imprison priests and harry their congregations—as in the Northern Counties after the Rising of 1715. But the normal conditions under William, Anne and the Georges, were much more favourable. There exists a long report of the year 1710, made to

Cardinal Paolucci in Rome, by one of his agents in the British Islands. The report states, in the most emphatic manner, that the Roman Catholics in England "enjoy the exercise of their religion totally free," that anyone who wishes can keep a priest in town or in country—and that no laws are enforced against Roman Catholics except those excluding them from office, and those making them pay double taxes. On the other hand, the same agent reports in detail how *in Ireland* the Roman Catholic body is cruelly persecuted, and the people are deprived of their religious rites in practice as well as in law. The report is well worth studying, as giving the contemporary point of view of Roman Catholics as to the difference of their treatment in the two British islands.[1]

English Roman Catholics were, however, until the period of Catholic Emancipation in the early nineteenth century, excluded from all part in the government of the country, local or central, and from sitting in either House of Parliament. Being inevitably Jacobite, they were inevitably suspect, and though they exercised their religion freely, they had to exercise it in private. They could not parade it; they could not in fact make propaganda. They remained in the eighteenth century under conditions in some respects more unfavourable than those of the Protestant Dissenters, who were the most stalwart of all the supporters of the governments born of the Revolution. Before the days of the Irish immigration into England, the Roman Catholics were an aristocratic community, held together on the basis of great Catholic households and their dependents; the "old religion" remained in the eighteenth century a gentlemanly creed, but unfashionable and secluded.

It was part of William's policy to treat all Protestants with equal favour. He hoped to obtain the abolition, as regarded the Protestant Dissenters, of those laws excluding them from civil office, which he approved in case of Roman Catholics. In short, he wished the Test and Corporation Acts repealed as regards Protestants. He even offered, if the Tories would consent to admit Dissenters to civil office, to allow in return the Non-juring, Jacobite Bishops to retain their Sees without taking the oaths of allegiance to himself—an offer of which the generosity is clearer than the prudence. But the Tories would not sacrifice the ark of their covenant for the sake of the Non-jurors and Jacobites. For the Tories believed the Church would

[1] It is in the Public Record Office, Transcripts, Rome, 101.

not be safe if Dissenters were admitted to civil office and political equality. The Whigs in Parliament did not press the matter hard. They themselves, as conforming Churchmen, could enjoy the sweets of office with the help of the nonconformist vote.

William's other desire was to see the Prayer Book so modified as to admit the more orthodox Dissenters within the pale of the Church. In this he was supported by Nottingham, the leader of the Church party in Parliament. But the clergy in Convocation pronounced strongly against it. Moreover, the Dissenters as a whole were lukewarm about the proposal; for in any case only some Dissenters— probably the Presbyterians—would find their way into the Church, and those who were still left outside, like Baptists, Quakers and Independents, would be, therefore, the more isolated and the more liable to be ill-used. It was for this reason that Locke himself, in the Preface to the *Letter concerning Toleration,* declared that Acts of Comprehension would "encrease our evil." So the scheme for "Comprehension," to enlarge the borders of the Established Church, fell through for want of support.

Thus, under the Revolution Settlement, the Puritans remained not only outside the Church, but theoretically at least excluded from Civil office. Since, however, Protestant Dissenters had always enjoyed the Parliamentary Franchise, and since religious toleration was now granted them, they were able to constitute the effective voting strength of the Whig party, and to exercise political influence on the Whig counsels and, therefore, indirectly on the counsels of the nation.

Such, in effect, was the religious compromise of 1689. It had the immense merit of giving peace to the land—a merit that far outweighs its logical defects, and its inconsistency with our modern theories of religious equality. Thanks to Holland and England, religious *toleration* began to have a place in the practice and in the thought of Europe. But religious *equality* was an idea that existed neither in the laws of European States nor in the minds of men. Just as the events of James II's reign made religious equality for Roman Catholics long impossible in England, so the memory of the events of the Cromwellian Revolution still made religious equality for Puritan Dissenters impossible. To have struggled for it would only have brought on fresh catastrophes. Thus the legal defences and monopolies of the Church of England on its two sides were not thrown down, but were positively strengthened by the reign of James II and the ensuing Revolution. At the same time, those events gave religious Toleration to Dissenters; and gave a great impetus to Latitudinarianism inside the Church, particularly on the Episcopal Bench. The Revolution, in its religious as well as its political aspect, was conservative and liberal at once.

The fundamental question at issue in 1688 had been this—Is the law above the King, or is the King above the law? The interest of Parliament was identified with that of the law, because, undoubtedly, Parliament could alter the law. It followed that, if law stood above the King's will, yet remained alterable by Parliament, Parliament would be the supreme power in the State.

James II attempted to make the law alterable wholesale by the King. This, if it had been permitted, must have made the King supreme over Parliament, and, in fact, a despot. The events of the winter of 1688-9 gave the victory to the opposite idea, which Chief Justice Coke and Selden had enunciated early in the century, that the King was the chief servant of the law, but not its master; the executant of the law, not its source; the laws should only be alterable by Parliament—Kings, Lords and Commons together. It is this that makes the Revolution the decisive event in the history of the English Constitution. It was decisive because it was never undone, as most of the work of the Cromwellian Revolution had been undone.

It is true that the first Civil War had been fought partly on this same issue:—the Common Law in league with Parliament had, on the field of Naseby, triumphed over the King in the struggle for the supreme place in the Constitution. But the victory of Law and Parliament had, on that occasion, been won only because Puritanism, the strongest religious passion of the hour, had supplied the fighting force. And religious passion very soon confused the Constitutional issue. Puritanism burst the legal bounds and, coupled with militarism, overthrew law and Parliament as well as King. Hence the necessity of the restoration in 1660 of King, law and Parliament together, without any clear definition of their ultimate mutual relations.

Now, in this second crisis of 1688, law and Parliament had on their side not only the Puritan passion, which had greatly declined, but the whole force of Protestant-Anglicanism, which was then at its height, and the rising influence of Latitudinarian scepticism—all arrayed against the weak Roman Catholic interest to which James had attached the political fortunes of the royal cause. The ultimate victor of the seventeenth-century struggle was not Pym or Cromwell, with their Puritan ideals, but Coke and Selden with their secular idea of the supremacy of law. In 1689 the Puritans had to be content with a bare toleration. But law triumphed, and therefore the law-making Parliament triumphed finally over the King.

But the supremacy of law could not be permanently secured if the Judges who interpreted it remained dependent upon the Crown. James had dismissed the Judges who refused to interpret the law as he wished. The Revolution secured the independence of the Bench.

One of the first executive actions of William, as King charged with the administration, was to make the Judges irremovable. This he did of his own free will, without waiting for a Bill on the subject to be passed by Parliament. He gave commissions to all the Judges under the formula *quam diu se bene gesserint*—so long as they behave properly: no longer *durante beneplacito*—at the will of the King. Prior to the Revolution some Judges had sometimes held under the more secure tenure—*quam diu se bene gesserint;* but most had held *durante beneplacito,* and not a few had suffered dismissal for political reasons. Under William and under Anne the Crown could no longer dismiss Judges. It is true, therefore, to say that the great boon of the independence of the Bench was in practice secured at the Revolution. But this independence and irremovability was only put on a statutory basis when the Act of Settlement, passed in 1701, came into force on George I's accession in 1714. The Act of Settlement lays it down that—

Judges' Commissions be made *quam diu se bene gesserint* and their salaries ascertained and established, but upon the address of both Houses of Parliament it may be lawful to remove them.

This only gave statutory force to what had been the practice of William and Anne since the Revolution; but the Act of Settlement added the power of removal by address of the Houses, as a safeguard against the Judges abusing their irremovable position. Under that tenure our Judges hold office to-day.

The station of Justice outside and above the sphere of politics was very largely achieved by the irremovability of Judges. The law was made arbiter of all issues by its own legal standards, without fear of what Government could do either to Judge or to Juries. It is difficult to exaggerate the importance of this as a step towards real justice and civilization. It has not yet been taken, or else it has been abolished, in many countries abroad, where "justice" is still a part of politics and an asset of despotism. But in England the old Tudor idea of the Judges as "lions under the throne" ceased to hold good at the Revolution. Henceforth they were independent arbiters between Crown and subject, acting on standards of law and of evidence. Nor had they ceased to be agents of royal policy, merely in order to become agents of Whig or Tory faction. Judges, like other men, are no doubt often influenced by their own opinions on party questions. But they were not dependent on Whig or Tory Governments, for they could not be removed by them. Under William and Anne, it happened not infrequently that Tory Judges thwarted Whig Governments, and Whig Judges thwarted Tory Governments by their action on the Bench.

Since public justice was henceforth to be impartial and no longer a mere instrument of the Crown, the law of Treason was altered by Statute in 1695 much to the advantage of the accused. He was to have a copy of the indictment. He was to be defended by Counsel. He was enabled to compel the attendance of witnesses for the defence. An overt act of Treason had to be proved by two witnesses. Henceforth, for the first time in our history, judicial murder ceased to be an ordinary weapon of politics and government.

This improvement in the realm of political justice was part of a more general movement in the direction of humanity and of scientific justice that was slowly setting in and which culminated in the nineteenth century. In the course of the eighteenth century there grew up a comprehension of the real value of evidence, and of the valuelessness of certain types of evidence like that of the professional informer—Oates, for instance. This improvement in the intelligence and justice of the law courts was noticeable not only in trials of a political character. In cases of every kind, the rules of the law of evidence—what evidence may be received in court and what may not—were worked out by the law courts during the eighteenth century. Sir John Holt, Chief Justice of the King's Bench under William and Anne, introduced a new regime of humanity and fairness towards the accused. The days of Scroggs and Jeffreys were over.[1]

Owing to the experience of James's tyranny, the "liberal" element

[1] Stephens, *History of Criminal Law*, Chap. XI; Holdsworth, *History of English Law*, VI, pp. 518–19.

in the Revolution Settlement was as much approved by the Tories as by the Whigs themselves. The reduction of the personal power of the King, the supremacy of Parliament and of law, the independence of the Judges, the security of the rights of individuals and of chartered Corporations against the encroachments of executive power were causes highly popular with the Tories of 1689. In the last years of Charles II, the Tories had, in their anger against the Whig Parliaments, spoken and acted as extreme Royalists and had made over to the King powers which they were fain to recall after their experience under James. Never again was the Tory party a Royalist party, in the sense of being a party anxious to increase the Royal Prerogative, for they never again found a King entirely to their liking, till George III ascended the throne. The High Tories soon found grounds of discontent with William III, and, contrary to their expectation, with Anne after him, and still more with George I and II. And therefore, for seventy years after the Revolution, the High Tories never recovered that enthusiasm for the wearer of the Crown which they had felt in the last years of Charles II. For this reason the reduction in the power of the Crown effected at the Revolution continued to be approved by all parties in the State. And when at last in 1760 a King agreeable to Tory sentiment ascended the throne, it was too late to revive the old Prerogative. No attempt was made to resuscitate the powers of the Stuart Kings. George III, devoted to the Protestant ascendancy, was only too faithful to the letter of the Revolution Settlement. All that he attempted was, with the consent of Parliament, to recover for himself those powers which had been left to the King in person by the original Settlement of 1689, but which had been exercised by the Whig Ministers under the early Hanoverian Kings.

But although, after the Revolution, the subjects of the land had little to fear from kingly despotism, they might fear the encroachments on liberty of new masters, the Houses of Parliament and the Government of the day armed with Parliamentary support. But this danger was mitigated by the division of Parliament into Whig and Tory, wherein lay security for the freedom of the subject under the new regime. The rivalry of the two parties made it certain that the Whigs would take up the cause of anyone oppressed by a Tory Government or a Tory House of Commons, and that the Tories would champion the humblest victim of Whig tyranny. There are a hundred instances of the working of this law of political dynamics in the reigns of William and Anne, besides the well-known cases of the Kentish Petitioners, the men of Aylesbury, and Dr. Sacheverell, and the failure of the Impeachments of Somers and of Oxford. The Revolution may have made Parliament dangerously powerful but, fortunately for freedom, Parliament continued to be a body divided against itself.

And so it proved in the important matters of the freedom of the press. The right of printing and publishing matter obnoxious to the Government of the day was secured as a result of the Revolution and of the continued rivalry of Tory and Whig. Hitherto, as in other countries so in England, it had been necessary to obtain licence from the authorities before printing and publishing any book, pamphlet or newspaper. There had, of course, been secret presses, which being illegal were usually conducted by the more violent opponents of Government, often in a very scurrilous manner. But open and legitimate discussion, whether on religion or politics, had been hampered by a rigid censorship. As a consequence of the spirit of the new age ushered in by the Revolution, this form of governmental control was abolished in 1695. In that year, the same year as the improvement in the law of Treason, the annual act for the Censorship of the Press was allowed to lapse and has never since been revived.

After this great emancipation, authors and publishers still ran, as they still run, the risk of trial for sedition or for libel before a jury of their countrymen. Without that safeguard, "liberty of the Press" would become an intolerable nuisance. The abolition of the Censorship is what is meant by a "free Press." It was that for which Milton had pleaded in his *Areopagitica, or the Liberty of Unlicensed Printing*. In that magnificent pamphlet, half poetry, half politics, occurs the famous patriotic brag—"What does God but reveal himself to his servants, and, as his manner is, first to his Englishmen?" It would have pleased Milton to know that England would be, in fact, the first great country to obtain a free Press, fifty years after the appearance of his *Areopagitica*. The violence of party in his own age, with which he himself was deeply infected, rendered freedom of speech or of printing at that time impossible. "Liberty of unlicensed printing" came in, not with Pym or with Cromwell, but as an outcome of a more peaceful and conservative revolution. For the

Revolution Settlement of 1689 was not the triumph of a party, but an agreement of the two chief parties to live and let live. The balance of Whig and Tory, each jealous of the other and both jealous of the Crown, served to protect the liberties of the individual Englishmen from the onslaughts of power.

VI   THE PERMANENCE AND GROWTH OF
THE REVOLUTION SETTLEMENT

Since the great place occupied by the Revolution Settlement in English history derives from its permanence as the root of our subsequent constitutional growth, a glance forward at later events is necessary in order to understand its full import. The Revolution produced a form of government and a trend of thought both of which lasted with little change until the era of democratic reform in the nineteenth century; and even then thought and practice were not reversed, but enlarged to suit a new age.

The Settlement of 1689 was not, so far as England was concerned, a mere party or sectarian triumph, but an agreement between parties and Churches to live and let live. In England, though not in Scotland or Ireland, the Jacobites who were thrust out of the scheme of government were only a small portion of the community. The new regime—Monarchy controlled by Parliament—was eminently suited to both Whigs and Tories, and the classes of society and types of thought and feeling which those two parties represented. The English Revolution made no such cleavage as the French Revolution permanently made in the national life. It reconciled more than it divided.

Under William and under Anne, government was mixed Whig and Tory; under the first two Georges it was Whig; and under George III and IV it was predominantly Tory once more. Throughout this long period, from 1689 to 1828, no essential change was made in the laws and customs of Church and State, except the development of the Cabinet and the office of Prime Minister as links between Crown and Parliament, and the growing tendency to regard

Ministers as responsible for every political act of the Crown. In the first part of this era the Whigs were foremost in defending the Constitution against the Jacobites, and later on the Tories in defending it on its other side against the "Jacobins," as the Radicals were called; but all along it was the same Constitution. The eighteenth century was the most conservative in modern English history as regards the institutions of the country, central and local—too conservative in fact, considering that the Industrial Revolution began half-way through this long period of institutional stability and stagnation. Social change outpaced political sameness.

Why did the Kings never again attempt to recover the lost Stuart Prerogative? Why should these laws of 1689, why should this Declaration of Right, be respected by the successors of James II, any more than he had respected other and no less explicit laws? What, in short, were the ultimate sanctions of the Revolution Settlement?

In the first place, the repercussion in men's minds and memories of so great an event as the Revolution, in itself constituted a security. The exile of James was a warning to English Kings and their advisers, and was never forgotten.

In the second place—no military force could be kept on foot without parliamentary sanction. The Army was still under the orders of the King, and its officers were still chosen by him, but he could maintain it only by annual application to the House of Commons. The Declaration of Right had laid it down:

That the raising and keeping a Standing Army within the Kingdom in time of Peace unless it be with the consent of Parliament is against Law.

That was merely a repetition of the old law which James had broken. But in effect the control of Parliament, and particularly of the Commons, over the Army was extended yet further as a result of the Revolution; it was extended to times of war as well as to times of peace. The way in which parliamentary control of the armed forces of the Crown was enforced, was twofold. The King was never again, in peace or in war, given money enough to keep up an army for more than a year. And the Mutiny Act, by which, in April 1689, Parliament enabled him legally to maintain discipline among his soldiers by Courts Martial, was passed for seven months only, till the next session; it has, ever since, been annually renewed by parliamentary vote. If the King omitted to summon the Houses for a single year, the Army, unpaid and without discipline, could no longer be kept on foot.

The Parliament that fought Charles I had for that purpose claimed command of the forces by sea and land. But the statesmen of the Revolution, once they had got rid of James, had no need to revive that highly unconstitutional claim. They had no need to coerce William by armed power; they had other holds over him, and were content therefore to leave undisturbed the direct obedience of soldiers and sailors to the Crown. Personal loyalty to the King remains the law and the tradition of the Army. It is his health, not Parliament's, that is drunk every night in the mess-room. It is the King's coat the soldier wears, and it is the King who gives his commission to its officers. Yet Parliament, since 1689, has seen all this without fear or jealousy, because it knows that there would be no army at all if the King ever broke with the Commons House. Indeed, after the Revolution the Whigs were less suspicious of a standing army than the Tories.

William and Anne, because they were trusted and supported by Parliament, were able to fight a long and ultimately successful war against the great strength of France. England's efficiency was doubled by the Revolution, without that loss of our domestic liberty which had been the price of Cromwell's power in the counsels of Europe.

This greater efficiency of England in war and in foreign affairs was the result, not merely of the new arrangements about the Army, but more generally of the co-operation of Parliament and Crown, which had been so signally lacking during the reigns of the Stuart Kings. Above all, it was due to the greater readiness of the House of Commons to vote money for wars and foreign policies which it approved and which it could control, as it had not been able to control foreign policy at the time of Charles II's Treaty of Dover. Indeed, the financial system that arose after the Revolution was the key to the power of England in the eighteenth and nineteenth centuries. It was also the chief sanction of the Revolution Settlement. No King after James II has ever been in a financial position even to attempt to break the law or to quarrel seriously with the House of Commons. Even George III, at the time when he was most unpopular in the country, had the House of Commons on his side, voting him supplies; and directly he lost his majority in that House, his personal control of government came to an end.

The Tudors and early Stuarts had tried normally to live on their own revenues and on grants for life that the Commons made to each King at his accession. The meeting of Parliament was not an annual but an occasional event. Only now and then did Elizabeth or Charles I have to apply to the House of Commons for special aid. So, too, Charles and James II had each at their accession had large revenues voted to them for life, and although these life revenues were not in themselves sufficient, Charles II, by the help of gold from the King of France, was able at the end of his reign to avoid summoning Parliament for four years, and James II for three years.

Warned by these experiences, the Commons took good care that after the Revolution the Crown should be altogether unable to pay its way without an annual meeting of Parliament. William had no large grant made him for life. Every year he and his Ministers had to come, cap in hand, to the House of Commons, and more often than not the Commons drove a bargain and exacted a *quid pro quo* in return for supply. Money was not voted till the King had made some concession, or withdrawn his opposition to some measure or policy which he disliked. This process, being now annual instead of intermittent, rendered the Commons masters of the Crown's policy, and led ere long to a result not foreseen by anyone in 1689, the selection of the King's Ministers on the new principle that they should be of the same party as the majority of the House of Commons.

The Commons after the Revolution voted money more readily, not only because they had more constant control over the action of the King's Ministers, but also because they were no longer afraid of the misappropriation of supplies. A machinery was established which prevented money from being spent on any purpose except that for which it was voted. A certain sum, indeed, was voted to William for his own use—the beginnings of the modern "civil list." But the rest of the money, far the greater part of the year's supply, was appropriated to one purpose or another by the votes of the Commons. The accounts were carefully scrutinized by Committees of the House of Commons; and woe to the Minister who used any sum for other purposes than those assigned by the appropriation. The House, in fact, had now got control in detail of the finances of the country and was therefore much more liberal in its votes of money than before the Revolution. The struggle for appropriation of supply had been going on in Charles II's reign. After the Revolution it was a closed question. The machinery of the House of Commons' control of finance was complete. And that was a main reason why the financial position of government improved so much after the Revolution. The Commons had no longer the motive to keep the King short, which had operated so disastrously for the national finances in the days of Charles I and II.

But the taxes were not voted on the irresponsible motions of private members. The Treasury officials of William, or of Anne, drew up a scheme for the year's taxation, and those of them who had seats in the House proposed it to the Commons. These proposals were not, as in later times, collected in a single all-inclusive Budget-bill. But none the less, each tax proposed to the House fitted into a general plan drawn up by the Treasury. Several of the most important Treasury officials, like Sir Stephen Fox and William Lowndes, were members of the House and took an active part in the lobbying and debates. So fully was this system recognized that at the end of Anne's reign the House passed the famous Standing Order No. 66 (as it is now enumerated). This famous rule of the House prevents money from being voted for any purpose except on the motion of Ministers of the Crown.

Ministers and Treasury officials were thus brought into direct contact with the legislators, explaining, defending and modifying the policy they advocated as experts, to suit the criticisms of the country squires. The squires on their side were trained by these conferences in the arts of statesmanship and the science of finance, and learnt to appreciate the needs and methods of government. Under this peculiarly English system, the Crown, the Ministry and the Treasury were all attached by leading strings to the House of Commons—but whether the House was leading, or being led, it was not always easy to say. It was an altogether admirable arrangement, the basis of sound finance, honest administration and free government. The mutual confidence of legislative and executive, secured by this elaborate machinery of mutual control, rendered the House of Commons generous in their grants of money, in striking contrast to the niggardly supplies which their fathers had doled out to Charles II, in days when members had only a very irregular control over the purposes, policies and persons whereto the money voted would actually be applied.

So, too, the debts of Government were ceasing to be personal debts of the sovereign and were becoming the national debts, contracted with the consent and on the credit of Parliament. During the wars against France, the debt rose by leaps and bounds, but its increase was not fatal, as our ancestors were always expecting it to prove, because it was well funded on a sound system guaranteed by Parliament. It was the National Debt, no longer the King's debt. A King might easily be made bankrupt, like Charles II: but it would take a lot to make the nation bankrupt.

Government borrowing on Parliamentary security, the National Debt, and the Bank of England founded in 1694, these were the methods and institutions that enabled England to defeat France and enlarge her Empire as much by the purse as by the sword; without Lord Treasurer Godolphin, Marlborough could not have won his wars; and without the financial support of the City and the House of Commons all Pitt's genius would not have won Canada and India. The system of Government borrowing was made easier by the fact that the "monied interest" was attached by political affection to the Governments born of the Revolution. Generation after generation we find the City magnates, many of whom were Dissenters, opening their purses to the secure investment of the National Debt guaranteed by Parliament, to support Governments they trusted. Their predecessors had not been so willing to lend to Charles and James II on less good security for ends they had grave reason to suspect.

All these things made for the strength of England at home and overseas. In 1688 France was not only a much more populous and wealthy country than England, but in the opinion of the world was greatly superior in political and financial organization. But after the English Revolution our political and financial system made our Kings in effect richer than all their rivals, while French finance and monarchy held the downward path towards the crash of 1789.

In everything to do with finance the House of Commons was now supreme, and this supremacy was very naturally extended to the cognate subject of control of trade. The Crown was now deprived of an old prerogative power, the granting of trade monopolies: in 1693 the House of Commons passed a resolution that all subjects of England had equal right to trade to the East Indies unless prohibited by Parliament. William did not venture to challenge this resolution, which took away from the Crown one of its chief sources of independent revenue and influence, the power to create trading monopolies as Elizabeth and the Stuart Kings had done. The charter of the new East India Company, and of all monopolist companies, like the East African Company, henceforth had to derive from Parliamentary Statute. Henceforth capitalist companies and merchants, like the great Josiah Child and his rivals of the Free Trade, must look no longer to the Court but to Parliament, and must make or mar their fortunes by intriguing and bribing in the lobbies of Westminster instead of in the antechambers and closets of Whitehall. This is a very characteristic and important example of the shift of power made by the Revolution, which affected every sphere of national life.

Hitherto, since Norman and Plantagenet times, "the Court" had been the heart of England, through which the various currents of her life-blood flowed. The best and the worst had always been found "at Court," struggling in the whirlpool of ambition and intrigue that surrounded the person of the sovereign. The Bishop, the lawyer, the religious reformer, the man of fashion, the gambler, the learned author, the poet, the playwright, the soldier, the sailor, the explorer, the artist, the merchant, the agricultural improver, the needy nobleman seeking monopolies or confiscated lands, the scientific inventor, the financial promoter, the scandalmonger and the common swindler all sought patronage at Court. Wherever the King moved, he drew after him this train of expectants. The life at Court was a microcosm of the nation's life. So it had been under Elizabeth, when as Touchstone said, not to have been at Court was to be damned. And so it still was in the Whitehall of Charles II.

All this ended at the Revolution. Power and patronage passed largely to the House of Commons and to the Peers of the Realm. And at the same time, under a cold preoccupied Dutchman, succeeded by the invalid Anne, the Court lost its social and fashionable importance even more rapidly than its political power. The Palace became, and has since remained, the secluded domestic shelter of our hard-working Kings and Queens, where public servants are daily interviewed and where, on State occasions, the doors are thrown open to a crowd of carefully selected visitors on their best behaviour. But it has never since the Revolution been the thronged and public centre of English life.

The House of Commons was the residuary legatee of the old Court. The House could hardly indeed be the centre of fashion, art and literature, in the same way as the Court had once been, but these activities found patrons, first among the aristocracy and later in the general public. The abolition of the Censorship helped to free the author from the need of courting "the great," though in Queen Anne's reign the Whig and Tory politicians enlisted the chief writers of the day to serve as party poets and pamphleteers.

But the post-Revolution House of Commons succeeded to the King's Court as the place where wealth and power were to be won. The Ministers chosen by William, Anne or George, could govern the country only if they kept the Commons in good humour. And so the social and monetary value of a seat in the Commons went up by leaps and bounds. Ever since the Long Parliament had asserted the power of the Commons, its individual members had been courted and often bribed. Charles II and Louis XIV both kept members in their pay. After the Revolution, the King of France ceased to be a serious competitor, but the King of England and his Ministers had more than ever to use direct and indirect bribery of the Commons House. Government paid members in places and sinecures; merchants and merchant companies paid them in shares or cash down. The most vital and the most corrupt spot in England in former times had been Whitehall; now it was Westminster. Where the carcase is, there will the eagles be gathered together.

With all its disadvantages and dangers, party spirit at least served to mitigate corruption. Whigs and Tories, each with their one-sided idealism and factious loyalty, preserved an incorruptible core of zealots, ready to bribe but not to be bribed. So long as the party fight was kept up with vigour, as it was throughout the reigns of William and Anne, so long as real and vital controversies were at issue, public opinion had great influence over the House of Commons, and corruption and self-seeking were kept at least within certain limits. But when, under the first two Georges, the Tory party, divided on the dynastic issue, broke up and sank beneath the surface, the element of sincere party rivalry on real principles came to an end for forty years (1720-60). During this period of the Walpole and Pelham regimes, parliamentary government was conducted by coteries of Whig magnates, divided only by personal rivalry in the scramble for place and power. Under the pacific government of Walpole "every man had his price," for public opinion, fairly contented with his tolerant rule, left the politicians to do very much as they liked.

During this period of political lethargy was perfected the business of borough owning and borough-mongering, by which individual Lords and gentlemen acquired, in effect, the power of nominating members for the "rotten boroughs." In Walpole's time the "rotten boroughs" were mostly in Whig hands; in the reigns of George III and IV they mostly were in Tory hands. But whichever party was its chief beneficiary, it was essentially the same system, until it was swept away by the Reform Bill of 1832.

In the last half of the eighteenth century the Commons House had become less representative of the real political forces in the country than it had been in the reigns of William and Anne. The geographic shift of population and the growth of new classes, hastened by the Industrial Revolution, were not registered by any change in Parliamentary Representation, until the long-overdue Reform Bill. Yet we must not exaggerate. There was never a close oligarchy; if the country was thoroughly roused it could make its will effective even in the unreformed House of Commons. Thus at the General Election of 1831, held on the issue of the Reform Bill, a majority of 120 was returned to abolish the rotten boroughs. The unreformed House of Commons reformed itself. There was no need of a second Revolution.

From 1689 to 1832 the power of the Crown was still very great, working within the fixed legal limits and accepting frankly the dependence of executive on Parliament. William and Anne both attempted to govern by mixed Ministries of Whig and Tory together, but it was soon found necessary to form Ministries of one party only, the party that could command a majority in the House of Commons. Party became the medium through which alone the King's government could be carried on under the Hanoverian Kings. But the power of the Crown, as the fountain of honours and patronage, was still strong enough to enable the King to choose which of the two rival parties he would keep in office. George I and II chose Whigs; George III and IV more often chose Tories. For the power and patronage of the Crown was enough to determine the result of a General Election as between the equally matched forces of Tory and Whig; and whenever those parties were most equally matched the Crown had most independent power. The Whig Chancellor, Cowper, wrote a memorandum for George I on his accession (1714) which contained the following significant words:

Give me leave to assure your Majesty, on repeated experience, that the parties are so near an equality, and the generality of the world is so much in love with the advantages a King of Great Britain has to bestow without the least exceeding the bounds of law, that it is wholly in Your Majesty's power to give which of the two parties you please a clear majority in all succeeding Parliaments, by showing your favour in due time, before the elections, to one or other of them.

The Chancellor, in short, had learnt from "repeated experience" under Queen Anne that the patronage of the Crown could decide general elections as between Whig and Tory. This was rendered possible by the small numbers of the electorate and by existence of rotten boroughs owned by single persons, whose support Government would buy with titles and posts. When the Reform Bill of 1832 supplied the constituencies with more numerous and more independent electors, Crown or Ministerial patronage could no longer decide electoral results. The Crown fell out of the political game. It became necessary instead for parties to bid against each other with legislative proposals intended to persuade or bribe whole classes. It was possibly an improvement; it was certainly a change.

It will be seen, therefore, that under the Revolution Settlement the wearer of the Crown still had great power, though it had to be carefully and prudently used, and no government policy could be carried on against the wish of the House of Commons.

In September 1913, when the question was raised, at the time of the Home Rule crisis, whether the King could constitutionally dissolve Parliament against the wish of his Ministers, Lord Esher wrote for the benefit of George V a memorandum in which occur the following words:

Has the King then no prerogatives?

Yes, he has many, but when translated into action, they must be exercised on the advice of a Minister responsible to Parliament. In no case can the Sovereign take political action unless he is screened by a Minister who has to answer to Parliament.

This proposition is fundamental, and differentiates a Constitutional Monarchy based upon the principles of 1688 from all other forms of government.

This is perfectly true. The responsibility of Ministers for all the King's political acts has held good from the beginning of Victoria's reign to the present day, and Esher was right in saying that it was "based upon the principles of 1688." Nevertheless, it was not established in so rigid a form at the date of the Revolution. On the whole, the Revolution did more to limit the Royal Prerogative than to transfer what was still left of it from the hands of the King to the hands of his Ministers; that consequential change came gradually as the years went by.

For example, William III still exercised at his own free will the important prerogative of changing his Ministers and dissolving Parliament.

In 1690 and again in 1701 he exercised these prerogatives contary to the wish of his most important Ministers and contrary to the wish of the House of Commons of the day; yet the electorate on both occasions endorsed his action at the subsequent elections. Anne did the same in 1710, and George III in 1783 with equal success. William IV did the same in 1834, but the subsequent General Election went against him. Since then no monarch has attempted to change his Ministers against the wish of the House of Commons, or to dissolve Parliament against the wishes of the Ministers.

It appears, then, that the remaining prerogatives of the Crown, as limited by the Declaration of Rights at the Revolution, did not pass in their entirety from the King's hands to those of his Ministers until the accession of Victoria. Yet Esher was right in ascribing the present complete responsibility of Ministers for all the King's political actions to the principles of 1688; it was from those principles that the rigid modern practice has been gradually evolved under pressure of the new conditions that the Revolution created.

Although the balance had settled down in 1689 on the side of Parliament, our Constitution was still, as our ancestors loved to call it, a "mixed" Constitution, of King, Lords and Commons. Each had a defined and important place in the working of Government from 1689 to 1832.

What, then, was the place of the House of Lords under the Revolution Settlement? Had the King's Ministers, in order to hold office, to make terms only with the Commons House? At the present day such is the case, both in appearance and in reality. And throughout the eighteenth century it was so, in appearance at least. It was the Commons who voted supplies to William and Anne, and could bargain for their terms. For awhile, indeed, the principal Ministers still sat in the Lords, till Walpole saw where real power lay, and preferred to rule the country from his seat in the Commons (1721-42). It was the Commons, not the House of Lords, whose vote sustained or dismissed Cabinets. The last fierce attack and defence of the Walpole Ministry (1741-2) was fought out, month by month, on the narrow floor of St. Stephen's Chapel. When at length Walpole's majority in the Commons disappeared, he resigned office, and retired to the Lords, saying in chaff to his old enemy Pulteney, whom he met in the dignified calm of the Upper Chamber, "My Lord Bath, you and I are now two as insignificant men as any in England."

From this it might be inferred that the Lords were no longer important. But, in reality, they had a considerable hold over ministries from the Revolution till the Reform Bill of 1832, because individual Peers returned so many members of the House of Commons at election time under the rotten borough system. This aristocratic control of elections increased as the eighteenth century went on, and partly for that reason there was less conflict between the two Houses of Parliament under the Hanoverian Kings than there had been under William and under Anne; under the first two Georges the majority in both Houses was always Whig, and under George III and IV generally Tory. So the harmony of the two Houses of Parliament continued, alike under the Whig and Tory regime, until the next great trial of strength between Lords and Commons over the Reform Bill of 1832 showed decisively where ultimate strength lay.

The eighteenth-century House of Commons consisted mainly of landed gentry, but of gentry in close touch with other interests besides land. Many of the leading professional men, especially lawyers, great merchants, army officers, and a few men of mere genius like Burke, found their way into the House. An ambitious and able Englishman had usually two aspirations: to become a Member of Parliament, and to acquire a landed estate. And so the House of Commons, though mainly an assembly of landowners, was none the less a fair epitome or representation of the educated and influential classes, although it was elected under a very odd and haphazard system.[1]

The Whigs represented mainly the wealthier landowners, the Dissenters and the mercantile community; the Tories mainly the squirearchy and Church. But in fact, the noisy battle between the Tory "landed interest" and the Whig "monied interest" was to a large extent a matter of party cries and shibboleths. It made little difference to policy. In practice, the Whigs did not neglect the land, nor did the Tories neglect trade. Throughout the eighteenth century, whichever side was in power, the House of Commons and the Cabinet took

[1] See Namier, *The Structure of Politics at the accession of George II*, Chaps. I and II.

into full consideration the economic requirements of all the upper and middling classes. The "poor" were neglected, as they always had been in every country and under every system of Government, until the rise of democracy as a consequence of the Industrial Revolution.

This was the system that Disraeli retrospectively called "the Venetian oligarchy"—whenever the Whigs were in office. Professor Namier, who has recently made a profound study of the political methods and persons of the mid-eighteenth century, denies that the governing families were "oligarchs," in the sense of aristocrats born to the purple. He says they were courtiers and parliamentary experts. They rose by their abilities in parliamentary debate, or parliamentary and Court intrigue. This was true even of the Duke of Newcastle, and it was as true of Walpole and the elder Pitt as it was true of his son or of Disraeli himself.

But whether or not the system of government was an "oligarchy," its methods were the opposite of Venetian. The methods of the oligarchy in Venice were despotism, inquisition, enforced silence and secret police. But the Whig rulers to whom George I and II entrusted the government, could only govern on condition of leaving the broadest freedom to their Tory opponents in accordance with the spirit of the Revolution Settlement. If they had provoked reaction, they, and the Hanoverian King with them, would have been overthrown.

The Whig "oligarchy" was submissive to the rule of law, as every Government has been since 1689. And the Common Law of England gave to the Executive no power of putting down public meetings or political writings that attacked Government. Unless a judge and jury would find a critic of Government guilty of sedition, Government could do nothing to silence him—except indeed give him a place! The Law Court, not the Government, decided what was libel; what was sedition; what was blasphemy. So it was in eighteenth-century England, and so it is to-day.

Throughout the eighteenth century, the legal character of civilization and politics in England is strongly marked. Blackstone's *Commentaries on the Laws of England,* first published in 1765, were favourite reading and had great influence not upon lawyers alone. The executive could not override the law, and that law was a law of liberty. The legislative could, of course, alter the law by passing new Statutes; but, in fact, Parliament in mid-eighteenth century legis-

lated very little, and not at all in the direction of curtailing the liberty
of the subject. Our modern criticism of that bygone regime and its
mentality is not that it interfered too much, like a Venetian oligarchy,
but that it interfered too little, allowing law to grow antiquated and
out of date, while society was being reshaped by industrial change.
Not tyranny but a supine conservatism was the weakness of Walpole
and the Pelhams after him. Walpole's favourite maxim *quieta non
movere* ("let sleeping dogs lie") is not the motto of a tyrant—but
neither is it the motto of a reformer.

When, in the course of George III's reign, Tory replaced Whig
rule, things continued in much the same way. Institutional change,
the reform of corporations, of Universities, of Parliament, of local
government was still neglected, though the Industrial Revolution
was making all chartered bodies in their old form more and more
out of date.

At the time of the French Revolution came the democratic movement under Tom Paine, demanding manhood suffrage. The mass of
opinion in the country was frightened into reaction, and the Tory
Government, backed by that public opinion, instituted more repres-
sive measures than the Whigs in their day had thought necessary or
safe.

But even in this era of anti-democratic repression in the time of
Pitt and Castlereagh, the Law and Constitution of 1689 were ob-
served. At the worst moments of "anti-Jacobin" panic, speech was
still free in the Houses of Parliament, though not in the country.
The most full-blooded orations of the opposition speakers in the
House of Commons, like Fox, were fully and freely reported by the
Press. Moreover, the repression of democrats in the country was carried on by ordinary process of law, through the verdict of juries.
When juries acquitted the accused Radical, Government had to let
him go free. So even the worst period of repression in England between 1790 and 1820 was very different indeed from Continental
methods of despotism, either past or present. And from first to last
it was the House of Commons who governed the country; and it was
the House of Commons who beat Napoleon, as it had beaten Louis
XIV. That was why, the moment Napoleon fell, the eyes of oppressed
Liberals in Europe turned to England as the home of ordered liberty, years before the Reform Bill was passed.

The Constitution from William III to George IV was not a perfect
form of government, but while it lasted Britain flourished more than

her neighbours, and it proved capable of peaceful readjustment to new conditions when the era of change at length came. "The principles of 1688" have been adapted and enlarged step by step to meet the needs of modern democracy.

Long use and custom have made liberty and peaceful self-government natural to Englishmen, and therefore they still survive the dangers of our own time. It is because the House of Commons has always governed the country since 1689, that it is able to govern us still, when popular assemblies of later birth have had their brief day and disappeared. It is because Englishmen two and a half centuries ago were set free to worship, to speak and to write as they pleased, that they are free still while so many others have again lost their less ancient liberties.

VII   THE REVOLUTION SETTLEMENT IN
SCOTLAND AND IN IRELAND

Our fathers, in disposing of the Crown of England and in making the Revolution Settlement for their own country, were not obliged to consider the wishes of anyone outside the borders of England and Wales. But the Revolution had its consequences in the other lands ruled by James, on the English Colonies, on Scotland and on Ireland.

The Colonies and Ireland were dependencies of England. The American Colonies, indeed, enjoyed domestic self-government in varying degrees. But economically and navally they were dependent on England, and had neither in law nor in practice any voice in the disposal of the Crown. It was only in 1931 that the Statute of Westminster laid down the very different doctrine that "any alteration in the law touching the Succession to the throne or the Royal Style and Titles shall hereafter require the assent as well of the Parliaments of all the Dominions as of the Parliament of the United Kingdom." But in 1689 no Englishman thought of consulting the Colonies on such high matters.

The deposition of James II was warmly welcomed by the great majority of the English-speaking Americans. Grave fears had been entertained oversea of the King's religious policy and his friendship with France, which in the Colonial mind was connected with the French of Quebec, the French Jesuits, and their Indian allies prowling dangerously along the ill-guarded western frontier. Moreover, James's absolutist tendencies in government came, in the last years of his reign, into violent conflict with the claim for a virtual Colonial independence, which, in Massachusetts at least, was as old as the Colony itself. The Revolution at home enabled the democratic parties of Massachusetts and New York to rise in successful revolt against the authority of Governor Andros. That able man had, under the orders of James II, curtailed self-government and suppressed the elective Assemblies. The object of James had been to effect a closer union of the separate Colonies in a "Dominion of New England"—a desirable policy in itself, but associated with a destruction of American liberties which must ere long have led to a fatal explosion. It is possible that, by putting a stop to these plans, the English Revolution postponed the American Revolution. It is certain that it relieved the violent tension between Colonial claims to self-government and James's assertion of the Royal Prerogative overseas.

Ireland, on the other hand, had to be reconquered before she would submit to the change of sovereigns. To the Roman Catholic majority of her inhabitants the Revolution meant not political and religious freedom but foreign domination and religious persecution. Of the Settlement which the Revolution imposed on Ireland by the sword, I shall speak more fully at the end of this chapter.

But Scotland was not in the same position as either the Colonies or Ireland. She was not subject to the English Parliament at all. She had a Parliament of her own, which was by law just as capable of disposing of the Crown of Scotland as the English Parliament was capable of disposing of the Crown of England. There were two separate Crowns, though they had rested on the same head ever since 1603, when James VI of Scotland had become James I of England. His grandson James II of England was James VII of Scotland. Britain was a "dual monarchy," and each of the two Kingdoms had its own law and law courts, Parliament, Executive and Church. In 1689 Scotland might have chosen to retain her King James VII, or to elect some person other than William and Mary in his place. But the Edinburgh Convention preferred to follow the example of the Convention at Westminster in the disposal of the Crown. In other respects, the Revolution Settlement in Scotland was necessarily diverged from the Settlement in England, for the circumstances of the two countries were widely different.

In 1689 no one could foresee whether the ultimate result of the Revolution in the two countries respectively would lead to a closer union of peoples and Parliaments, or to worse quarrels between Scots and English ending in ultimate separation of the Crowns. This question, on which the future power and welfare of Britain so largely depended, remained very urgent and very uncertain until the Union of the Parliaments was effected by agreement in 1707. And it was not immutably established until the final defeat of Scottish Jacobitism in 1745-6. But the first step towards a closer agreed union of the two peoples was taken in 1689, when the Scots Parliament repudiated the authority of James VII and invited William and Mary to become King and Queen of Scotland.

In order to understand the situation in Scotland at this epoch, and the wide difference between parties in Scotland and the parties bearing the same names in England, it is necessary to look back to the period of the Reformation. In the days of Elizabeth of England and Mary Queen of Scots, the countries they respectively ruled had adopted two opposite methods of imposing the will of the modern laity on the mediæval Church.

The Tudor Reformation in England preserved the mediæval organization of the Church intact—apart from the abolition of the Papal supremacy and the suppression of the orders of monks and friars dependent on the Pope. The foreign elements were removed, but the native part of the Church remained unaltered in its old organization, under Bishops, Archdeacons and higher clergy. The mediæval organization of the Church, which was preserved in modern England, gave no voice to the laity. Convocation consisted entirely of clergymen. The parish priest was responsible to no lay elders in his parish. All this purely clerical machinery the Tudor Reformation preserved; it instituted nothing like the English Church Assembly with its House of Laymen, a creation of the twentieth century.

None the less, the Reformation in England was an assertion of lay control over religion. And since in England the internal organization of the Church remained wholly clerical, it followed that the will of the laity had to be imposed on the Church from outside, by Crown and Parliament. That was the essence of the Tudor Reformation on its political side.

In Scotland, on the other hand, the laity and the Reformers had no chance of imposing their will on the Church either through the Crown, which rested on the head of the Roman Catholic Mary Queen of Scots, or through Parliament, which had not the prestige, the tradition or the machinery for the great tasks of the English Parliament. And so, in the days of John Knox, the Scottish laity, instead of controlling the Church from outside through Crown and Parliament as in England, entered into the Church themselves as a part of her self-governing machinery. The Reformation in Scotland changed the

Church into a democratic body—governed by a double democracy, a democracy of clergy or parish Ministers free from episcopal control, side by side with a democracy of laymen. The discipline was stricter than the episcopal discipline of England, and it was the discipline of a democracy of parish clergy and lay Elders.

The English Reformation was Erastian, that is to say the State controlled the Church: the Scottish Reformation was clerical and democratic. This difference in the methods by which the power of the Church of Rome was destroyed in England and Scotland respectively, led to a different method of fighting out the subsequent quarrels of the rival Protestant parties in the Stuart era. In England the battle about religion was fought out as a battle between Crown and Parliament. In England, from the reign of Elizabeth to the death of Cromwell, the Puritan or advanced Protestant party tried to impose its will on the Church through Parliament, while the Anglicans strove to impose their will on the Church through the rival authority of the Crown. This, more than any other cause, led to the Civil War between Crown and Parliament, on the question— does Crown or Parliament govern the Church? But the Church herself did not in this quarrel act independently as an ecclesiastical organization. The English Church did not, like the Scottish Church, set itself up as a third party to King and Parliament. The English Church was divided, and the rival schools of her clergy attached themselves to King and Parliament respectively. The High Church doctrine of the seventeenth century magnified not the political power of the Church but the political power of the Crown. The strength of the English Puritans, prior to 1660, lay in Parliament—not in the Westminster Assembly of Divines, whose function was only to advise Parliament. Erastianism is common ground to Cavalier and Puritan, to Tory and Whig. Englishmen, agreed in little else, were at least agreed that religion is to be settled by the State, not by the Church—by the King or else by Parliament—not by Pope, Bishops or clerical assemblies of any kind.

Very different was the procedure adopted beyond the Border. In Scotland there arose the powerful organization of the Kirk, democratic in machinery and in spirit, with the laity represented on an equality with the clergy both in the parish organization and in the Church Assemblies. This organization, to which there was nothing analogous in England, had been obliged to act as a principal in the political struggles of the day from its first inception by John Knox in the struggle with Mary Queen of Scots. The Reformed Church had to fight for itself or perish, because the Scottish Parliament was quite unable effectively to fight its battles, and could only register its decrees.

In the absence of an effective Parliament, the Church claimed to represent the Scottish people better than any other body. And it had undertaken the education of the Scottish people. Over against this otherwise all-powerful Kirk stood the Crown. The Stuart Kings asserted the power of the State against the Church, the liberty of the individual against the inquisitorial power of the clergy and lay Elders. When the Kings of Scotland became Kings of England, the Crown felt itself strong enough to defy the Kirk from Whitehall, when the whole power of England strengthened the arm of Scotland's King. Those of his Scottish subjects who objected to the Calvinist discipline, rigidly enforced by a popular priesthood, were numerous, especially among the nobles and higher gentry. Being unable to protect themselves against the clergy by help of Parliament as in England, they rallied to the Crown and formed the Scottish Cavaliers or Tories.

The Cavalier and Tory party in Scotland in the seventeenth century was the refuge of tolerationists, anti-clericals, gentlemen who disliked a democratic Church, and ordinary human beings who objected to having their lives dictated by the clergy and elders, and who disliked standing on the stool of repentance to be preached at before the congregation. The Cavalier or Episcopalian party in Scotland wanted to be free of clerical control, but they did not want to use the English Prayer Book—at least not till the eighteenth century. When Charles I and Laud tried to force the Prayer Book on Scotland, Montrose and the future Scottish Cavaliers temporarily joined with the Kirk against the King. On the Prayer Book issue the whole Scottish nation was against Charles I. The Covenant of 1638 was in one of its aspects a patriotic stand of all Scots for their religious and national independence against the English King. But in another aspect the Covenant registered the tyrannical resolve of the more religious people in Scotland to impose their will as a denominational body on all their fellow-countrymen, not only in matters of religion, but in questions of politics and of everyday life and conduct. The Scottish Cavaliers were opposed to the democratic, inquisitorial Church, not on grounds of liturgy or doctrine, but on social and political grounds.

To restrain the power of the Church Assembly and the Kirk Sessions, the Stuart Kings in Scotland revived the Bishops, much as the Duke of Wellington said that he re-introduced Chaplains into his regiments "to restrain the ravages of enthusiasm." Episcopacy in Scotland under James VI and I and again under Charles II implied no change of liturgy or doctrine; it was a change in Church government intended to curb the political and social power of the democratic Church. If, after the Restoration of 1660, the royal statesmen in Scotland had played their cards well, they would have represented the party of toleration and good sense against the intolerable claims of the clergy. But the reckless and inhuman methods of Middleton and Lauderdale on behalf of the Episcopalian establishment were on a par with the methods of the Presbyterian zealots whom they persecuted. The dragooning of the Scottish Covenanters and the military ill-usage of the whole population of the West under Charles II, left an ineffaceable mark on the imagination of Scotland and relieved the Kirk of much of the odium which it had incurred in the days of its former supremacy. Scott's *Old Mortality* tells the story of those unhappy times in its essential features.

Then round came the Revolution. It was caused in Scotland, as in England, by James II's attempt to restore the ascendancy of the Church of Rome, an anachronism that cut right across the established controversies of the seventeenth-century Scotland. The strict Presbyterians would not in ordinary circumstances have had the power to overturn the Government, in the face of the Episcopalian party, which was very strong, particularly in the East. But James II's conduct played straight into the hands of the Scottish Whigs and Presbyterians, who took the lead of the nation in the winter of 1688-9. The Tories and Episcopalians looked on in bewilderment, unable to support the Church of Rome, yet unwilling to strike at the King. The Scottish Tories did not put themselves in the forefront of the rising that resulted in the Revolution, as the English Tories did that winter. Partly for that reason the Convention, that met in Edinburgh in 1689 and called William and Mary to the throne, went much further in a Whig and Presbyterian direction in the final settlement than did the contemporary Convention Parliament in England. As the Scottish Episcopalians had taken no active part in effecting the Revolution, they did not share in its rewards.

The Scottish Revolution Settlement, made at Edinburgh while Claverhouse was raising the Highlands against King William, was

necessarily more partisan Whig than the English Revolution Settlement, which was made by an agreement of the representatives of
both parties. The Scottish Convention did not talk about "abdica-
tion." They boldly declared, in Whiggish terms, that James had "forfeited" the Crown. And they abolished Episcopacy, root and branch.
It is this absence of compromise in the Scottish Revolution Settlement
as distinct from the English which accounts for the continuance of
a strong Jacobite party in Scotland for two generations to come among
the formidable Episcopalians of the Eastern Lowlands.

The origin of Jacobitism in the Highlands was different. It was due
to the jealousy felt by the other clans and chiefs against the predominance of the Campbells, the Earls of Argyle. The Argyles had,
ever since the reign of Charles I, associated the interests of the
Campbell clan with the Presbyterian and Whig cause. It followed
that the neighbouring clans would only carry on the old tribal
vendetta by taking the side first of the Cavaliers and then of the
Jacobites. And so, in four successive generations, Montrose, Claverhouse and the old and young Pretenders were able to recruit Highland armies, and in course of time the romantic tradition of Jacobitism became an inherited passion among many of the Highland clans.

The Scottish Revolution Settlement of 1689 was made by the
Scots themselves. It was not dictated from Whitehall or from Westminster. The hard treatment of the Episcopalian clergy of the South-
West, who were "rabbled" by the Presbyterian mobs that winter in
revenge for the dragoonings of the previous twenty years, was done
against the wishes and interests of William, and aroused deep indig-
nation among his new Tory subjects in England. But neither he nor
they could interfere. Ireland was in Jacobite hands, England herself
was still in grave trouble, liquidating her own Revolution; and the
new Dutch King was in no position to alienate his only friends in
Scotland, the Presbyterian party, however much he might regret
some of their proceedings.

So the Convention Parliament at Edinburgh settled Scotland without interference from London. But its deliberations ran considerable
danger of rude interruption by Scottish claymores, coming from the
opposite direction.

> To the Lords of Convention, 'twas Claverhouse spoke,
> "If the King's Crown go down, there are crowns to be broke."

In the summer of 1689 Scotland was convulsed by the news that an army of Highlanders were moving down from the hills, under John Graham of Claverhouse, whom James had made Viscount Dundee. He was known as the best soldier in Scotland and the pitiless foe of Covenanters and Whigs. Above the pass at Killiecrankie, the primitive valour of the tribal swordsmen, not for the first or last time, proved more than a match for the half-evolved tactics of the modern musketeer. King William's Scottish army of regular troops was destroyed. But Dundee fell in the hour of victory, and there remained no officer with authority enough to inspire and control the fitful and quarrelsome energies of the Highland clans. Before they had fairly debouched into the plain and made contact with the Jacobites of the Lowlands, they were stopped by a single regiment of volunteers that had just been recruited among the covenanting peasants of the South-West. This small body of resolute enthusiasts, under their leader Cleland, defended the town of Dunkeld against the whole Highland host. The victors of Killiecrankie, who may with equal truth be regarded as an army of heroes and a band of marauders, lost heart at this first check, and melted back into the hills with their glory and their plunder, each man to his distant glen. The "Lords of Convention" could proceed again undisturbed with the task of settling the Scottish Church and State "on a Revolution basis."

But the difficulty of governing Scotland remained as great after the Revolution as before. The restoration of the Presbyterian system, to which the majority of the Lowland peasantry were attached, had indeed done much to pacify the South. Yet even there the more extreme covenanting zealots refused to acknowledge William because he was an "uncovenanted" King, and on this ground sometimes made common cause with their bitterest enemies the Jacobites. The Episcopalians were still the stronger party in the East Lowlands north of the Forth, and they were Jacobites to a man. For many years after the Revolution, Episcopalian clergy retained their livings and conducted service in one-sixth of the parish churches of Scotland.

If the power of the new government was weak even in the Lowlands it did not exist beyond the Highland line. The mountain clans were governed not by the King or law of Scotland, but by their own chiefs. Some of the clans, like the Campbells, were in alliance with William; some were Jacobite; some put up their allegiance for sale.

Scotland indeed was only half pacified; and there was another difficulty confronting the Governments of William and Anne which had been unknown to their predecessors. The Edinburgh Parliament had caught the contagion of liberty from the events of the Revolution. It had been a cypher under the Governments of Charles and James, but it now asserted itself as a force to be reckoned with. From 1689 till the Union of 1707, the Scottish Parliament had a much more independent and active career than at any earlier period of its not very glorious history.

Before the Revolution, the Scots Parliament had been in leading strings. From time immemorial a Committee known as "the Lords of the Articles," acting on behalf of Government, had the power to prevent Parliament from discussing any business save that which the Privy Council wished it to discuss. In 1689 the "Lords of the Articles" were abolished, and the Parliament was set free to debate any subject, and to pass any law it wished—subject only to the King's right of veto on legislation.

This was something new indeed, and it doubled the difficulties of government. Ever since the Union of the Crowns in 1603, Scotland, though nominally an independent kingdom, had in fact been ruled as a dependency of England by orders issued from Whitehall. The Scottish Privy Council had been nominated and instructed from London, and the Scottish Parliament had merely confirmed the decrees of the Privy Council. But the Revolution introduced a new spirit of independence into Scotland, and particularly into her Parliament. In the days of Lauderdale's misgovernment under Charles II, the Edinburgh Parliament had made no effective protest on behalf of the ill-used populations of the South-West. But in William's reign the Parliament took up the Glencoe crime and insisted on inquiry and exposure. A few years later, in the affair of the Darien colony, where the interests of England and Scotland came into collision, the Edinburgh Parliament boldly championed the national cause, defied the rival Parliament at Westminster and called in question the policy of the King. When the two Parliaments and peoples were thus openly at strife, the position of the unhappy wearer of the two Crowns became impossible. He was, as it were, divided against himself. Then finally in Queen Anne's reign the Scottish Parliament threatened to dissolve the Union of the Crowns; they declared that they would, as soon as the Queen should die, choose a King who should not be the same person as the Hanoverian successor in England. Such a King was not unlikely to be the Pretender.

The new spirit of independence that the Revolution had breathed into the Scottish Parliament made it impossible to preserve the system of the Dual Monarchy. Either England and Scotland must again have separate Kings, or else they must cease to have separate Parliaments. In Anne's reign the choice was happily made: the closer Union of the two Kingdoms was carried out by agreement between the two Parliaments to merge themselves into a single Parliament of Great Britain. It was a Treaty negotiated on equal terms between the two peoples who were to become one nation. The Union of 1707 left Scotland her own separate Church on the Presbyterian model, and her own law courts; and gave her the immense advantage of free trade with England and her Colonies. The English Empire, from which Scots had been excluded, became the British Empire in which they were to play so great a part. Scotland obtained very good terms at the Union, because she was formidable. Very different was the Union with subjugated Ireland in 1800.

The Union of 1707 had indeed heavy going for a generation after its passage, for it was unpopular in Scotland, and the Jacobites clamoured for its repeal. But after 1746 it proved an inestimable blessing and strength to both countries. It may be regarded as the ultimate form taken by the Revolution Settlement in Scotland. The need for a Union on equal terms was caused by the greater independence of Scotland resulting from the Revolution; and the Treaty of Union was carried by those sections in Scotland and in England who were interested in preserving the Revolution Settlement and the Hanoverian Succession against a Jacobite restoration.

The Settlement of Scotland made in 1689 put an end to the worst evils from which the land had long been suffering, but it was far from a perfect settlement. It had at least the merit of preparing the way for the Union, and so leading in the end to the era of real pacification and progress, material and spiritual, in the reign of George III. The age of Hume and Robertson, Burns and Scott was the golden age of Scotland, her poverty at last relieved and her former feuds softened down into matter for history and romance.

Ireland was the Achilles heel of the Revolution Settlement. Yet even in Ireland the arrangements made after the reconquest at the Boyne and Limerick lasted for ninety years unchanged. But they rested on a basis of force alone.

At the Restoration of Charles II in 1660, the order of things in Ireland had not been substantially changed. The worst part of Cromwell's settlement stood firm. Most of the land of Ireland (probably between two-thirds and three-quarters) remained in the hands of Protestant landlords, for whose benefit the native Catholic chiefs and owners had been extruded. But the peasants subjected to this alien rule continued in the Roman communion; it was the religion of the great majority that was depressed and proscribed. There were, however, a few districts where Protestant colonists of all classes had made a real occupation of the soil, particularly in Ulster, where they formed perhaps half the population. The Protestants of this flourishing colony were themselves divided between English and Scottish, or in other words between Anglican and Presbyterian. But in face of the common enemy, the Celtic Catholic population whom their ancestors had expropriated, all Britons and all Protestants could be counted on to act together.

When the Roman Catholic James II came to the throne, it was inevitable that the native population should rise against the Protestant ascendancy and the Cromwellian land settlement. On this occasion it was not necessary to rebel; for authority and law were now on the side of the Catholic Celts. James very soon decided to govern Ireland no longer through English Tories like Clarendon, but through James Talbot, Earl of Tyrconnell, a Catholic Irishman burning to destroy the Anglo-Scottish colony, and prepared if necessary to hand the island over to France. He "remodelled the corporations" of Ireland, as Charles and James II had done those of England. Hitherto all Catholics had been excluded from the government of the towns: now they were given a great majority, even in towns like Londonderry. The Bench of Judges suffered a like change and the laws began to be unjustly interpreted against Protestants: the boot in fact was now on the other leg. At the same time the militia and army were even more completely changed. The Protestant officers and men were dismissed and replaced by Catholics.

If, while the authority of James was still unchallenged, Tyrconnell's new Catholic army had been sent to occupy Londonderry and the other possible centres of Protestant resistance, the history of Ireland might have followed a different course. But James brought the strength of his Irish army over to hold down his subjects in England, and the Protestant Colonists in Ulster were therefore able to move in their own defence when the time of crisis came.

In December 1688 the news that a Revolution was proceeding in England aroused both sides in Ireland to acts of open warfare. The peasantry in thousands armed themselves with pikes, or received muskets and ammunition from Tyrconnell. The Protestants scattered throughout the island were in dismal plight; many of them were disarmed, plundered and imprisoned; all firmly though erroneously believed that a St. Bartholomew massacre was intended; crowds of fugitives escaped to England, while the bolder spirits rode sword in hand to join the centres of Protestant resistance in the North.

Four-fifths of the island, including the eastern or Belfast side of Ulster, was held by King James's forces. Only in western Ulster the men of Enniskillen and Londonderry proclaimed King William and made good his authority in their region, summoning the scattered Protestants of Ireland to rally round the flag they raised. They were men well fitted for war: an aristocracy bred to organize and bear rule, well-mounted horsemen, pioneers and men of their hands accustomed to guard their own heads amid a hostile population. In the spring of 1689 they had to stand alone without help from England, where the administration and the army were still in such confusion that William could send no help to Ulster. James, on the other hand, less than three months after his flight from England, landed in Ireland with French officers and a great store of arms and ammunition for the peasant recruits.

James, however, at this period of his life, always exerted a paralysing influence over military operations wherever he came. Instead of bending every effort to reduce Londonderry and Enniskillen before they could be relieved from England, he began to play at politics, as if the whole island were already his. In May 1689 he summoned a Parliament at Dublin. It contained only six Protestants. This assembly, which posterity has abused and praised to excess, acted as it was certain to act. It proceeded to reverse by legislation the Cromwellian Settlement, and to give back the land of Ireland from Protestant to Catholic hands, and passed a Bill of Attainder against some 2,000 persons. Half the energies and thoughts of Ireland were directed to these proceedings in Dublin, and the personal and political feuds they engendered among the Irish, French and English Jacobites. Only half the nation's mind was given to the reduction of the Northern Protestants.

In these circumstances the famous siege of Londonderry took place. From April to the last day of July 1689 the gallant population endured the attacks of a great army of besiegers, and the worst extremity of famine. They were relieved at the very last moment by a fleet from England. With the help of the boats' crews of H.M.S.

Dartmouth armed with axes, the merchant vessel *Mountjoy* broke the boom on the Foyle, and floated up with its food-laden consorts to the quayside of the starving city. The siege was raised at once. At the same time the men of Enniskillen, who had kept up a brilliant guerrilla war all this time, defeated 5,000 of James's troops at Newton Butler. A fortnight later the first large detachment of troops from England landed under the Duke of Schomberg, and eastern Ulster, including Belfast, was recovered at a blow.

In this way the Protestant colony in Northern Ireland was saved, largely by its own heroic exertions, which still exercise in memory a dominating influence on the poetical politics of its descendants.

But the year 1689 ended with the rest of Ireland still in the power of James. Posterity may be tempted to regret that it was not left in Irish hands, to which, after more than two centuries of blood and tears, it has reverted by the laws of nature. But in real history there are no such short-cuts by primrose paths. In 1690 no one on either side envisaged a "reasonable compromise" about Ireland. Indeed the government of James and Tyrconnell had made it impossible.

The English had no thought of compromise. The Tories were as eager as the Whigs to recover England's lost property. It was a Tory House of Commons that in 1690 equipped William with a large army to reconquer Ireland.

And on their side the Irish had no thought but to recover the whole island and to root out the hated Saxon; if James would serve this purpose he should be their King; otherwise they would do without him, for they had not, like the Scottish Jacobites, any personal loyalty to the House of Stuart. But in any case the alliance with France was essential to their success and military aid was sent by Louis in increasing quantity, including considerable numbers of troops.

Our ancestors, Whig and Tory alike, understood little of realities in Ireland, and thought it a light matter to convert, or at least to hold down, a whole nation by force. Here they were wrong, but in one thing they were right. They saw that an Ireland, independent and hostile and garrisoned by French troops, would be fatal to England. We were at war with Louis, whose great power was threatening all Western Europe with conquest. Our own distracted island stood in great danger from the French and Jacobite combination. In 1690 William's throne was tottering. If Ireland became a base for French armies, fleets and privateers, England would shortly be destroyed or compelled to take James back on his own terms. Every motive, good and bad, wise and foolish—greed, anger, patriotism, love of liberty and religion—impelled the English to reconquer Ireland. And William was the man to do it for them. To him the Boyne campaign was part of the great European struggle for religious and international freedom against France. Till the French were expelled from Ireland and their supporters there subdued, nothing could be done to check them on the Continent, and the Revolution Settlement in England remained in hourly danger. The reconquest, which meant slavery for Ireland, meant freedom and safety for England, and in the long run for Europe.

The international aspect of the war was well represented on the two banks of Boyne Water; on the northern shore, led on by the Dutch Stadtholder who was England's King, were mustered the English regiments and the Ulster colonists, detachments from half the Protestant countries of Europe, and the Huguenot refugees from France. On the southern shore were not only the tumultuous, ill-disciplined levies of Irish peasantry and the gallant Irish horse, but the white coats of French battalions.

The destruction of James's army that day (July 1, 1690), and his own too early flight first from the field and then back to France, put the victors in possession of Dublin and three-quarters of Ireland. The English Revolution was saved, and England had set her foot on the first rung of the ladder that led her to heights of power and prosperity in the coming years. And by the same action Ireland was thrust back into the abyss.

Deserted by James, but inspired by a new national leader, Sarsfield, the Irish rallied behind the broad natural rampart of the River Shannon. Limerick on the Shannon was besieged by William, but it was defended in the same spirit with which Londonderry had been defended the year before. The siege was raised, partly owing to the exploits of Sarsfield who raided the English line of supply. William had to return, leaving a quarter of Ireland unconquered. But next year (1691) the work was completed by his lieutenants, who forced the Shannon at Athlone, destroyed the Irish army at Aughrim, and compelled Sarsfield to capitulate after a second siege of Limerick.

The Treaty of Limerick, that thus put an end to the war of the Revolution in Ireland, permitted Sarsfield to carry to France, into the service of Louis XIV, those of his army who chose to go into exile. They and their successors became a valuable element in the

French armies fighting against England for several generations to come. "The wild geese," as they were politically called, flew over in flocks every year to serve abroad against their racial enemies, and no doubt this constant exodus of the most determined spirits was one of the reasons why Ireland itself remained for so long quiet under the alien yoke.

Another clause of the Treaty of Limerick promised that the Irish Catholics should continue to enjoy "the privileges enjoyed in the reign of Charles." These had been meagre enough, but even this miserable promise was broken. William did indeed attempt to prevent the grosser breaches of the Treaty of Limerick, and play the part that Charles II and his great Lord Lieutenant, Ormonde, had sometimes played in mitigating the lot of the subjugated Catholics. But since Charles's day the Revolution had reduced the Royal Prerogative, and made the English Parliament more completely master of Irish policy. And the English Whig and Tory members were at one with the Protestants of the Dublin Parliaments in their desire for plunder and vengeance. By 1700 the amount of land left to the Irish landlords had been reduced by further confiscations to little more than an eighth of the whole island. The class of Anglo-Irish Catholic landlords, who might have done so much to interpret between the two nations in time to come, was practically abolished by these measures of confiscation.

Similarly new penal laws, passed in the reigns of William and Anne, made the persecution of the religion of the majority worse than before. For some years a real attempt was made to extirpate Catholicism by depriving the peasantry of the rites of their religion, and preventing the Bishops from coming over to consecrate a new generation of priests. In the reign of George I this attempt was abandoned. As it became clear that the Catholics could not be converted, the activities of the priests were permitted to become more open. But the attempt to keep the land, the wealth, the education and the social power of the country in the hands of Protestants succeeded for several generations to come. The native upper and middle class was so effectually robbed and depressed, that the priest remained as the only friend and leader of the people. The outcome of Protestant legislation was to make Ireland the most priest-led country in Europe.

Though positive religious persecution gradually died out, the Catholics remained under civil and social disabilities of a peculiarly galling and degrading character. They were prevented from sitting in or voting for the Irish Parliament, from holding any State or municipal office, from practising at the Bar, from purchasing any land beyond that which they inherited, from possessing arms, from owning a horse worth more than five pounds. Any Protestant tendering five pounds could possess himself of the hunter or carriage horse of his Catholic neighbour. Such odious laws divided the Protestant from the Catholic and helped to foster the worst spirit of "ascendancy." It was only in the latter half of the eighteenth century that the latitudinarian and tolerant spirit of the age mitigated that spirit and began the long process of modifying and repealing the Penal Laws. By that time irreparable harm had been done.

From William to George III English statesmen and Members of Parliament thought of the Irish question in two lights—first, political and military; secondly, colonial and economic. And these problems were approached solely from the English point of view.

The political and military conundrum for England was how to hold Ireland safe from French invasion and Jacobite rebellion, how to prevent her from being made a place of arms for French attack on England and on England's commerce. And it was not easy to hold Ireland in war-time when the great majority of the inhabitants were Roman Catholic Jacobites, at heart in league with France. If they were allowed to grow rich, organized and educated they might with French help drive the English into the sea. They must therefore be kept poor, leaderless and ignorant. The cruel policy succeeded for several generations in its object. After 1691 there was no more fighting or rebellion. Not even in 1715 or 1745, when the Jacobites rose so formidably in Scotland, was there so much as a whisper of revolt in Ireland. These satisfactory results were attributed to the maintenance and renewal of the Cromwellian land settlement which placed the ownership of almost the whole island in Protestant hands, and to the Penal Laws which crushed the heart out of the Irish Catholics. As Swift said, they were politically "as inconsiderable as the women and children." So far the policy succeeded, but at what a cost to the future relations of the English and Irish peoples!

Secondly, English statesmen regarded Ireland as a colony, that is a place where commerce and agriculture were to be encouraged or checked exactly as best suited the interests of English farmers, manufacturers and merchants; for such was a colony in the mercantile philosophy of that age. And unfortunately the agricultural and industrial interests of Ireland happened to be precisely of the kind of which farmers and manufacturers in England were jealous. Ireland therefore suffered far more than the American colonies from English commercial restrictions. To please English farmers, the export of cattle to England was stopped by Charles II's Cavalier Parliament. We never dared to stop the similar Scottish cattle trade to England either before or after the Union. To please English business men, the Cavalier Parliament of Charles II also excluded Ireland from that partnership with England in the Navigation Act which Cromwell had extended to her. The Restoration statesmen excluded Ireland from trade with the Colonies, and the Revolution statesmen continued that policy. Finally, the Revolution statesmen added one last blow of their own; in 1699 the English Parliament passed laws restricting the exportation of certain kinds of Irish manufactured cloth to any part of the world. There was already a prohibitive tariff preventing its import into England. Now cattle farming, sheep farming and the cloth industry were essentially Protestant interests in Ireland. All of them were struck at by the English Parliament, in obedience to English commercial and agricultural jealousy, contrary to England's political interest, which was to foster the Protestant population in Ireland.

If we consider the Penal Laws against the Catholics of Ireland and the commercial laws of which the brunt fell on the Protestants of Ireland, we cannot be surprised that respect for the law has little place in Irish tradition and mentality.

Protestant Ulster was hampered by these commercial restrictions dictated by English commercial jealousy. The linen industry that was permitted because it did not compete with any great interest in England, was a poor substitute for cattle, colonial commerce and woollens. Many thousands of Irish Protestants migrated to America early in the eighteenth century, long before the Irish Catholic migration thither began. England prevented the Protestants bettering themselves in Ireland, and as the Protestant Scots and English were determined to better themselves, they went to America, carrying thither no kindly tradition about England.

In religion as in commerce the English rule in Ireland was most illiberal and had the effect of dividing the Protestant interest. While the Penal Laws crushed the Catholics, the Presbyterians were harassed by laws passed in the High Church interest. The Scottish Presbyterians of Ulster, the men who had closed the gates of Londonderry

in the face of James's army at the crisis of the Revolution, were under the Revolution Settlement treated as an inferior class, half-way in
the social and political scale between the downtrodden Catholic and
the Episcopalian of English origin who alone was a full citizen.

Not until 1719 was a Toleration Act for Irish Presbyterians at
last carried, legalizing the position of their public worship like that
of their co-religionists in England. And even then the good things of
State Patronage were reserved for Irish Churchmen, or for English
sent over to fatten on Ireland. The Irish Presbyterians lived throughout the eighteenth century under a sense of grievance and inferiority,
which their proud stomachs could not easily endure. They were not
worse off than Nonconformists in England but they were more formidable and therefore resented their grievances more. It was this
angry tradition among the Presbyterians that gave such force to the
anti-governmental movements in the last twenty years of the eighteenth century.

Now the basis of all this variegated ill-usage, commercial and religious, of the inhabitants of Ireland of all races and religions by
England, was a constitutional point of the first importance—the
power claimed and exercised by the English Parliament and Privy
Council over the Irish Parliament and administration. Irish administration was entirely subject to the will of English Ministers, and
they kept the best places in Irish Church and State for Englishmen.
For a hundred years after the Revolution, no Irishman was Chancellor of Ireland, and the best places in Government were reserved
for men from England. Even the Episcopalian Churchmen of Ireland, though they possessed a monopoly of posts in Church and
State as against Catholics and Presbyterians, enjoyed in fact only the
leavings of Irish patronage, which was used to paying the party
debts of English statesmen to their own followers at Westminster.
Irish patronage in Church and State was regarded as a useful adjunct
of the English party system of spoils for the victors.

Furthermore, the English Ministry had control of Irish legislation
also, under the old Poynings Law of Henry VII. "The ultimate form
which every Irish measure assumed was determined by the authorities in England, who had the power either of altering or rejecting
the Bills of the Irish Parliament." And the Irish Parliament, "though
it might reject the Bill which was returned to it from England in an
amended form, had no power to alter it." Moreover, the English

Parliament itself legislated freely for Ireland, over the head of the Dublin Parliament, as when it prohibited her export of woollen goods to the Continent, or passed the Schism Act of 1714 to suppress Presbyterian Schools in Ireland.

The protest against this constitutional bondage of Ireland to England was made successively by four men in four successive generations. All of them were Protestants, but all carried with them the whole body of popular opinion of all creeds in their protest on behalf of Ireland. These four men were Molyneux, in the reign of William, Dean Swift in the reign of George I, Flood and Grattan in the early and middle years of George III.

These four successive protests of Molyneux, Swift, Flood and Grattan are marked by a graduated scale of importance and formidableness, till the last protest, Grattan's, took shape of the actual revolution of 1782.

Molyneux, who began the movement in William III's reign, merely wrote a pamphlet which was condemned by the English House of Commons. It set men talking and no more. But it set them talking on a theme they never again forgot. For Molyneux claimed the full and sole competence of the Irish Parliament to legislate for Ireland, on a footing of equality with the English Parliament. The subservience of the Irish Parliament and administration to England he declared to be an English usurpation. Ireland was a separate Kingdom, belonging to the same King as England, but not a conquered country. If the Parliament at Westminster is to legislate for Ireland, said Molyneux, Ireland must have her representatives in an Imperial Parliament. The flaw in Molyneux's argument is that in 1690-1 Ireland—in the sense of Catholic Ireland—had actually been conquered by England, and was indeed a conquered country, conquered at the Boyne and Aughrim. The most effective English answer to Molyneux would have been —"If you Irish Protestants want to be independent of the English Parliament and Ministry, we will withdraw our troops and our ships, and the Catholics will rise on you and cut your throats." Indeed, such an answer was indicated by Sir Charles Davenant and other English writers of the day. So long as the Irish Protestants intended to maintain the Penal Laws and the Protestant Ascendancy, they were in fact dependent on England, whatever the truth of the historical and legal argument might be. It was only when in Grattan's day the Irish Protestants began a policy of conciliating the Catholics,

that they were in a position to enforce Molyneux's doctrine of independence in face of England, as they did in 1782.

Till that year the Revolution Settlement for Ireland remained unaltered. It was, as we have seen, one of the worst settlements ever
made, of which the best that can be said is that it was only a prolonga-
tion and strengthening of a bad system already in existence. It was
exactly the opposite in spirit of the Revolution Settlement in England, for it represented the mere spirit of conquest and arbitrary
power.

CONCLUSION

The Revolution gave to England an ordered and legal freedom, and through that it gave her power. She often abused her power, as in the matters of Ireland and of the Slave Trade, till she reversed the engines; but on the whole mankind would have breathed a harsher air if England had not grown strong. For her power was based not only on her free Constitution but on the maritime and commercial enterprise of her sons, a kind of power naturally akin to freedom, as the power of great armies in its nature is not.

In the affair of the Revolution the element of chance, of sheer good luck, was dominant. It was only the accident of James II that gave our ancestors the opportunity to right themselves. At the end of Charles II's reign nothing seemed less probable than that England would soon become either a powerful state or a free and peaceful land. The violence of her factions for half a century past had reduced her to prostration before a royal despotism in the pay of France. One of two things seemed certain: either the system would continue unchallenged till all religious and political Dissent had been crushed out of existence and till France had conquered Western Europe; or else another turn of the tables, possibly another civil war, would produce another violent overturn, but no true "settlement." Nothing could really have saved England except the apparently impossible— a reconciliation of Tory and Whig, Church and Dissent. That miracle was wrought by the advent of James II, who united against himself the old antagonists. The eleventh-hour chance thus given to our ancestors was neither missed nor abused. For they established a new regime tolerable to all the great parties who had opposed the policy of James. The settlement therefore involved real "liberty of the sub-ject," not merely liberty of a victorious faction, which is all that most Revolutions can produce in the way of freedom.

It was a victory of moderation, a victory not of Whig or Tory passions, but of the spirit and mentality of Halifax the Trimmer. No doubt the element of "moderation," which the Revolution en-throned, had been latent somewhere in the English nature all along, but between 1640 and 1685 it had seldom won its way to the surface of affairs.

The Settlement of 1689 was in its essence the chaining up of fanati-cism alike in politics and in religion. Religion in those days was the chief motive of politics, and after the Revolution a movement to-wards latitudinarianism in religion enveloped first England and then for a while all Europe. This latitudinarian movement, of which the origins can be traced in Charles II's reign in the Royal Society and the Broadchurch theologians, was one of the causes of the reason-ableness of the Revolution Settlement, because the men of 1689 found the idea of Toleration less abhorrent than it had seemed in 1640 and 1660. And one of the chief results of the Revolution was the wide extent and long duration of the latitudinarian influence in the eighteenth century. After a last outburst of Church fanaticism at the end of Anne's reign in the Sacheverell affair and the Schism Act, the spirit of religious persecution withered and died in the Hanoverian atmosphere. "Enthusiasm" became bad form among the governing classes. And even the "enthusiasm" of Wesley was not an armed and persecuting creed like the earlier Puritanism. Living in an age of Toleration, the Wesleyans had no need to assert their tenets by force. The new Puritans were not tempted to cut off the head of the Archbishop of Canterbury, for Laud's mild successors did not deny them the right to hold as many Coventicles as they pleased.

In the mid-eighteenth century, religious fanaticism was moribund, and the fanaticism of class and of race had not yet arisen to vex mankind with new ills. During this blessed breathing space between the English and the French Revolutions, Englishmen learnt by the passage of quiet years the difficult art of leaving one another alone. And the King and his subjects, governors and governed, also learnt to abide by the law, in that most legal of eras.

These engrained habits of toleration and respect for law sank deep into the English mind during the hundred years that followed the Revolution, and had their effect when the stresses of a new era began

—with the democratic movement, the French Revolution and the social problems of the great industrial change. The habit of respecting constitutional rights acted as some check on the violence of the anti-Jacobin reaction, and the same habit of mind carried the Radical and working-class movements into legal and parliamentary channels. The victims of the Industrial Revolution at the beginning of the nineteenth century sought a remedy for their ills by demanding the franchise and Parliamentary Reform instead of general overturn; this happy choice was due in part to our national character but largely also to our national institutions, in which the oppressed saw a way of escape. The English Revolution had the ultimate effect of saving the Crown and much else besides.

The great emollient of the common ills of life, the humanitarian movement in all its aspects, began in the eighteenth century before the issue of democracy was raised. Judged by our modern standards, the eighteenth century was rough and cruel, especially to the poor, but it was less rough and less cruel than any previous age. It saw the Charity School movement, the first imperfect attempt to give a smattering of education to the great masses of the people as distinct from a few clever boys; the improvement in medical and hospital provision which enormously reduced the high death rate that all previous ages had accepted as a law of nature; Howard's investigations of the facts of prison life; the anti-slavery campaign; the movement for the mitigation of harsh laws and cruel punishments. Many of these things the nineteenth century carried out, on lines laid down by the eighteenth-century pioneers of thought and mercy.

This great humanitarian movement, to whose sphere of operations there is no limit, was a new birth of time. It arose in the milder atmosphere of the great religious and party truce which the Revolution Settlement had ushered in. It could not have arisen if the feuds of the Stuart era had been carried on in their full intensity into later generations.

The ultimate view that we take of the Revolution of 1688 must be determined by our preference either for royal absolutism or for parliamentary government. James II forced England to choose once for all between these two: he refused to inhabit any half-way house. It was as well that the choice had to be made so decisively and so soon; for the compromise system of the Restoration, though very useful in its day, had led to weakness abroad and constant strife at home.

The system of government by discussion has its disadvantages, under which in new forms we are labouring to-day, in face of absolutist governments of a new and more formidable type than those of Europe of the *ancien régime*. But if, on the balance, we prefer the path on which our feet are planted, we must commend the choice that was made once for all at the English Revolution.

INDEX